Understandin

TRAVEL &
HOLIDAY HEALTH

Dr Gil Lea & Bernadette Carroll

Published by Family Doctor Publications Limited
in association with the British Medical Association

IMPORTANT NOTICE

This book is intended not as a substitute for personal medical advice but as a supplement to that advice for the patient who wishes to understand more about his or her condition.

Before taking any form of treatment YOU SHOULD ALWAYS CONSULT YOUR MEDICAL PRACTITIONER.

In particular (without limit) you should note that advances in medical science occur rapidly and some of the information contained in this booklet about drugs and treatment may very soon be out of date.

© Family Doctor Publications 1997–2003
Updated 1998, 2002, 2003

Family Doctor Publications, PO Box 4664, Poole, Dorset BH15 1NN

Medical Editor: Dr Tony Smith
Consultant Editor: Chris McLaughlin
Cover Artist: Dave Eastbury
Cartoonist: Dave Eastbury
Design: MPG Design, Blandford Forum, Dorset
Printing: Reflex Litho, Thetford, using acid-free paper

ISBN: 1 898205 93 0

Contents

Introduction

Almost 60 million holiday and business trips are taken abroad each year by people from the UK, and it's inevitable that some travellers will become ill or have accidents while they're away. Some of these people will need immediate medical attention, while others can wait until they get home before seeing a doctor. A few will feel well when they first get home, and only start to feel ill some time later.

Most of the illness and accidents that affect travellers are preventable, at least to some extent. The aim of this book is to explain the potential hazards and offer you some practical advice on how you can keep these risks to a minimum. Some advance planning and commonsense precautions while you're away can make all the difference between a successful holiday or business trip and a medical nightmare.

Planning ahead

CHOOSING THE RIGHT HOLIDAY

For anyone planning a package holiday, the range of options on offer is almost mind-boggling. It's as easy to get to distant tropical destinations as it is to the Mediterranean and, although some brochures supply information about possible health hazards, others still provide virtually none. The organisers of activity or adventure holidays usually give some guidance as to the level of physical fitness required, but, even if you're considering a relaxing beach holiday or a sight-seeing tour, it's worth giving some thought to the possible stresses involved.

Some of them aren't obvious until you think about them. For example, if you're flying directly into airports at high altitude – such as those in the Andes in Peru,

Ecuador or Bolivia – you need to check that the itinerary allows you time to acclimatise to high altitude before much physical activity or further ascent is necessary.

Even without altitude problems, very busy itineraries may result in the holiday being far from restful, particularly for elderly or less fit people. Sometimes travel companies are tempted to cram too much into a relatively short time to attract clients who want to see the maximum in a limited holiday period. Once committed to the itinerary, travellers who find it too arduous may be unable to make last-minute alterations.

If you're pregnant or travelling with young children, you need to think extra carefully about any possible health risks, especially malaria. The disease is more dangerous in pregnancy and high-risk malarial areas are unsuitable destinations during pregnancy.

Some anti-malaria tablets and immunisations against other diseases may not be suitable so make proper enquiries before you book. It's a good idea to check with your GP if you're in any doubt whether the holiday may complicate any existing health problems, and you could also take the opportunity to top up your supplies of any medication you need to take regularly.

Tropical climates are a major attraction when it comes to beach holidays, but bear in mind that high humidity may be uncomfortable, even when you're planning to be thoroughly lazy. It's worth checking out the likely hours of sunshine and humidity as well as the temperature and rainfall before finally settling on your destination. It is also worth checking on the World Health Organization (WHO) website (www.who.int/en/) for any major disease outbreaks and very rare advice not to travel. This happened with the severe acute respiratory syndrome (SARS) in south-east Asia in spring 2003.

In these days of increased security warnings against terrorism, it is sensible to check the advice on political stability and safety given by the Foreign and Commonwealth Office (see Useful information, page 103). Even for the many destinations where there are no travel restrictions, it is sensible to be aware of any personal safety issues in the country to be visited. If you have any reason to be concerned, it's useful to know you can get advice on political stability and traveller safety from the Foreign and Commonwealth Office which has been running its 'Know Before You Go' campaign (see 'Useful information' on page 103).

TRAVEL INSURANCE

As well as covering you for any medical expenses abroad, travel insurance normally includes theft or loss of your baggage as well, and you would be foolish to risk going away without it. Unfortunately, it can be expensive so if you're on a tight budget it's tempting to economise and rely instead on the reciprocal health care arrangements between the UK and European Union and some other countries. Although these are useful, they cannot replace proper travel medical insurance.

First, fewer than a third of countries world-wide have any type

of agreement with the UK. Second, even those that do make no provision for getting a patient home in an emergency, nor do they provide any help towards an escort travelling or repatriation of a body should someone die overseas. Nevertheless, even given these limitations, the agreements can sometimes be useful. Details of arrangements with individual countries are given in the free booklet *Health Advice for Travellers* (T6), available from the Department of Health (see 'Useful information' on page 102). It also contains the application form CM1 and form E111 which you need to prove your entitlement to treatment. The forms have to be completed and taken into a post office for checking and stamping before travelling. They are valid indefinitely for short visits abroad by a UK resident, but you must remember to take them away with you.

Virtually all tour operators offer travel insurance policies which you buy at the time of booking and many travel agencies offer a similar service. Before agreeing to either, make sure you read the small print carefully. Some policies specifically exclude 'dangerous activities' such as motor cycling, scuba diving or parasailing. Extra premiums may be required for winter sports. There may be exclusions for pregnancy, age and accidents involving alcohol and drugs. Nearly all insurance policies exclude pre-existing medical conditions (see page 47). You will need to inform them of any such condition and request them to confirm in writing whether they have agreed. This situation can otherwise lead to disputes. Another circumstance that is usually excluded is any claim arising from an act of war or terrorism. Currently, a very small number of companies will cover these issues, so it is worth shopping around. You should also read the section on repatriation arrangements and check the amount of cover you're buying. You need to be sure that it's adequate for your destination, bearing in mind that medical costs in countries such as the USA are extremely high.

In most cases the insurance company will provide a 24-hour assistance telephone number to be contacted before any major medical decisions are made. Ask for and keep all receipts for any medical treatment or medicines obtained abroad in case you need to make a claim when you get home.

ALL ABOUT IMMUNISATIONS

The words 'vaccination' and 'immunisation' have come to be used almost interchangeably, although vaccination originally only referred to the smallpox vaccination. The term 'vaccination'

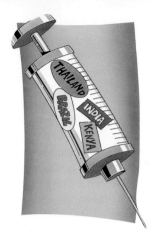

is used by the World Health Organization (WHO) to describe the other internationally required certificates of vaccination against yellow fever and, in the past, cholera.

Immunisation is a more modern term and covers the production of immunity (or protection from infection) in two ways. In 'active' immunisation, the body believes that the virus or bacteria in a vaccine are an attack from a real disease and after about a week the body 'actively' produces its defence antibodies, which will then be ready for an encounter with that disease. In 'passive' immunisation, the antibody (part of the body's defence system against infection) itself is injected (for example, gamma-globulin used in the past against hepatitis A) and the body 'passively' receives some instant protection. This 'borrowed' protection lasts less time than protection built by the body itself.

These days there are very few immunisations that are compulsory. In other words international certificates of immunisation are required only to enter a small

OF COURSE I'M VERY WELL TRAVELLED JUST LOOK AT MY IMMUNISATIONS!

KENYA 95, INDIA 94 GOA 93, TURKEY LAST YEAR!

number of countries when you're travelling direct from the UK. These are some of the countries within the potential yellow fever disease zones across Africa from west to east and also the north part of South America.

A yellow fever vaccination certificate is required from all travellers for entry to some of these countries, even straight from the UK. For others, the certificate is not required for entry on a direct flight, only if your journey is via another country within the yellow fever zone. Otherwise, there are no other international certificates required by the International Health Regulations. At one time, smallpox and cholera certificates were necessary to cross most borders beyond Europe, but the eradication of smallpox, and the fact that immunisation against cholera does not stop the international spread of the disease, have resulted in them no longer being required.

One other mandatory requirement does exist, in excess of the International Health Regulations. Proof of immunisation against meningococcal meningitis has been required for all those going on the pilgrimage to Mecca in Saudi Arabia since 1988. This regulation was introduced following an outbreak of the disease, exacerbated by the huge influx of people from many corners of the world.

Apart from these mandatory requirements, other immunisations may be advisable but are not compulsory. Frequently these optional immunisations are important for your own protection but attempts to find out what you need may end in confusion.

Some foreign embassies and tourist offices in this country who are anxious to encourage visitors may well tell you that you don't need any immunisations.

This is literally true in that no certificates are required to enter the country for travellers coming from the UK. It does not necessarily mean you don't need to consider getting yourself protected against certain health risks before you go.

Where to get advice

Increasingly, responsible tour operators are putting a few lines on health precautions in their brochures or booking forms and some travel agents will provide a little advice. However, you shouldn't expect them to tell you precisely which malaria tablets and optional immunisations you should have, although they will warn you about mandatory certificate requirements.

Once you've decided which country you're visiting, you should consult your GP or a specialist travel clinic for travel health advice. In fact, an even better option is to make preliminary enquiries before you finally make up your mind about your destination as the answers may influence your decision.

A useful booklet worth consulting before you book is *Health Advice for Travellers* (T6) produced by the Department of Health. You can get a free copy on request (see 'Useful information' on page 102). It contains advice on health topics as well as forms E111 and CM1 (see page 4 on health insurance).

Arranging your immunisations

Travellers often worry that they may have left it too late to obtain full protection. In fact, while it is ideal to start in plenty of time, especially for long overland trips, some useful protection may be worthwhile even a day or two before departure if necessary.

For a major journey including rural areas it is wise to start about six to eight weeks before you travel so that immunisations against diseases such as rabies and Japanese encephalitis can be spaced over a month and be completed at least 10 to 14 days before you leave. The interval allows time for the vaccine to become effective and for any reaction to have settled. Yellow fever immunisation takes 10 days to become fully effective and for the certificate to become valid.

For most package holidays to the Mediterranean or to the main resorts in the Far East, taking your immunisations about two or three weeks before your trip will suffice. Although the vaccine for hepatitis A takes at least two weeks to become maximally effective, it is believed to provide some useful protection even a few days before travel. This is because the incubation period of the disease is three to six weeks, which allows the vaccine protection to be building up, and so taking the vaccine late is better than omitting it completely. A second dose 6 to 12 months later prolongs the protection for about 10 years and prevents the late immunisation situation arising again – very useful for the growing number of last minute bookings. If necessary you can have it right up to your departure date. As hepatitis A is the most common disease in travellers for which an immunisation exists, it should allow 10 weeks, where possible, before travelling for their first course of immunisations. For repeated trips, this will not apply.

Side effects

Everyone seems to have heard scare stories about bad reactions – either the pain of the injection or the after-effects appear to get magnified with the telling. Of course older people, particularly men who served in the armed forces some years ago, do remember times when the needles became blunt with re-use and the vaccines caused more reaction. The

is worth considering even at this late stage if you're going anywhere with poor food and water hygiene conditions.

Middle-aged and older people and anyone else who did not receive childhood immunisations old TAB (typhoid and paratyphoid A and B) jab, sometimes combined with cholera, was famous for causing the recipient to feel very ill for a day or two, sometimes with a temperature and generalised aches and pains.

The new vaccines are more purified, often containing just the required part of the organism, and this results in fewer reactions. In fact nowadays it is uncommon to suffer much, usually just a tender area on the arm and only occasionally a little tiredness or mild under-the-weather feeling.

The actual injection is done with a sharp, fine needle and this reduces the discomfort a great deal. People are often surprised to learn that they have received several immunisations when they only really felt one. In time, more vaccines are likely to be swallowed in liquid or capsule form.

Even gamma-globulin, which was the injection people liked least (probably because it was given into the buttock), was not nearly as bad as the stories would have you believe. Even so, most people are greatly relieved to hear that none of the travel vaccines currently available is given into the buttocks.

Some people – mostly young men – are prone to fainting after injections. This is very rarely anything to do with what was actually in the injection, but more a reaction to the fact of being injected. As people become more used to having immunisations as an adult, and find that they are not as terrible as they feared, they gradually overcome the tendency to faint.

If you know that you're one of the fainting sort, you can help yourself (and the doctor) by ensuring that you have eaten something before you attend for immunisations. It also helps to lie down while the immunisations are being done and for a little while afterwards. This will usually stop you fainting and help to build up your confidence.

Egg allergy

Before you have any immunisations, you may be surprised to be asked whether you are allergic to egg. The reason is that some vaccines (including yellow fever, tick-borne encephalitis and 'flu) can contain minute quantities of egg. This might mean you couldn't have the vaccines if you have a true egg allergy, but if you don't eat them simply because you don't like them or they give you indigestion, you can still go ahead.

You should discuss any allergies (including penicillin) with the doctor but they are rarely a problem in practice. Urticaria or an allergy to bee and wasp stings may mean you shouldn't have the Japanese encephalitis vaccine.

Nevertheless, in the unlikely event that you do experience a severe or possibly allergic reaction after any immunisation, you should tell the doctor before you have any further ones.

Vaccines you may need: the basics

● **Tetanus:** everyone should have had a basic course of vaccine against tetanus. Travelling is an opportunity to check. This is particularly important for older people who may have missed out on a childhood course. A booster will be recommended for those travelling to developing areas who received a basic course over 10 years ago. It is also important for those travelling to remote areas or camping, when medical treatment may not be available. Tetanus is caught by bacterial spores from soil or dirt getting into a wound – even a fairly minor one.

Nowadays, tetanus vaccine is always combined with diphtheria vaccine.

● **Diphtheria:** this vaccine is routinely given to babies, to children when they start school and to school leavers. However, adults born before 1940 may have never been immunised and they should be protected. Younger adults may need a booster for outbreak areas and also for longer stays in developing areas. The vaccine can be given separately or combined with tetanus vaccine.

● **Polio:** protection is generally advised for travel outside northern and western Europe, the USA and Canada, Australia and New Zealand. The WHO is progressing with the global eradication of polio, which is hoped for by 2005. Routine childhood immunisation will continue for a few years longer.

Certification of polio eradication has already been declared in Central and South America, so polio boosters are no longer necessary for travel there. The disease has almost gone from large areas of south-east Asia and the vaccine will be gradually recommended for fewer areas throughout the world. Polio, or more correctly poliomyelitis, was once known as infantile paralysis. However, it can affect adults who are not immunised (usually those who were born before 1958).

The three vaccines above are included in the routine childhood immunisation programme which reminds us that one of the ways some diseases are kept at bay is by the great majority of people being immunised in childhood. In countries where immunisation programmes do not reach everyone, the risk may be higher. Any travellers who have not completed their courses should enquire about doing so.

● **Tuberculosis (TB):** those without a BCG scar (from immunisation against TB, usually on the upper outer side of the arm) should enquire about a test to see whether they need immunisation with BCG. This may be advised for longer trips to developing countries, particularly for anyone who is staying with families or working in such areas. It is not usually necessary for ordinary holidays

staying in international style hotels.

Extras for certain areas
The general recommendations for each geographical area do not vary very much and the main guidelines can be given here. However, it's important to get up-to-the-minute advice on the country you're going to before you leave as there may have been alterations to the international yellow fever regulations published annually by the World Health Organization (WHO), new vaccines may have become available or there may have been recent disease outbreaks.

● **Yellow fever:** yellow fever immunisation is only needed for travel to or through a yellow fever endemic zone (see maps). A certificate may be required (check with a yellow fever centre) and this becomes valid after 10 days and lasts 10 years. Even if a certificate is not required, currently the WHO recommends immunisation for all travel to countries where there is risk of yellow fever, particularly if you'll be travelling outside the main cities. A certificate should be provided when the immunisation is performed.

Many, but not all, GP practices are yellow fever immunisation centres, but if not they can supply you with the address of one in your area. There are specialist travel

Areas of Africa where yellow fever may be a risk

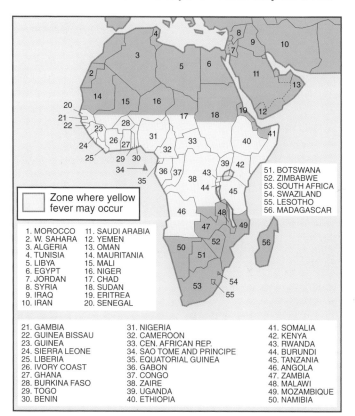

Zone where yellow fever may occur

1. MOROCCO
2. W. SAHARA
3. ALGERIA
4. TUNISIA
5. LIBYA
6. EGYPT
7. JORDAN
8. SYRIA
9. IRAQ
10. IRAN
11. SAUDI ARABIA
12. YEMEN
13. OMAN
14. MAURITANIA
15. MALI
16. NIGER
17. CHAD
18. SUDAN
19. ERITREA
20. SENEGAL

21. GAMBIA
22. GUINEA BISSAU
23. GUINEA
24. SIERRA LEONE
25. LIBERIA
26. IVORY COAST
27. GHANA
28. BURKINA FASO
29. TOGO
30. BENIN
31. NIGERIA
32. CAMEROON
33. CEN. AFRICAN REP.
34. SAO TOME AND PRINCIPE
35. EQUATORIAL GUINEA
36. GABON
37. CONGO
38. ZAIRE
39. UGANDA
40. ETHIOPIA
41. SOMALIA
42. KENYA
43. RWANDA
44. BURUNDI
45. TANZANIA
46. ANGOLA
47. ZAMBIA
48. MALAWI
49. MOZAMBIQUE
50. NAMIBIA
51. BOTSWANA
52. ZIMBABWE
53. SOUTH AFRICA
54. SWAZILAND
55. LESOTHO
56. MADAGASCAR

THESE GUIDELINES CHANGE FROM TIME TO TIME.

clinics in most main cities which can also provide this immunisation (plus the others if required).

● **Cholera and travellers' diarrhoea:** this disease is still common in areas where hygiene is poor, but the traditional injected immunisation against it is not very effective and is virtually never given these days. There are no remaining official requirements for an international certificate and any unofficial demands should be met by obtaining a medical certificate of exemption. Such demands for cholera certificates become more uncommon each year and, it is

Areas of South America where yellow fever may be a risk

1. PANAMA
2. COLOMBIA
3. VENEZUELA
4. GUYANA
5. SURINAM
6. FRENCH GUIANA
7. ECUADOR
8. PERU
9. BOLIVIA
10. PARAGUAY
11. CHILE
12. ARGENTINA
13. URUGUAY
14. BRAZIL
15. FALKLAND Is.

Zone where yellow fever may occur

CHECK THE CURRENT SITUATION BEFORE TRAVELLING.

hoped, will soon cease altogether. Most travellers are at very little risk from cholera. A new vaccine combining cholera with ETEC (enterotoxigenic *Escherichia coli*), one of the most common forms of travellers' diarrhoea, may become available here in late 2003/early 2004. The vaccine has been used in Scandinavia where it is considered to provide some protection against cholera for two years in adults and against ETEC for three months. The vaccine is not used in children under two years of age. It is taken as a drink. Two doses are needed pre-travel, at least one week apart. It is possible that the authorities in this country will only license the vaccine for use against cholera. However, the idea of a vaccine to prevent travellers' diarrhoea is very attractive. It must be remembered that ETEC is not the cause in all cases and the vaccine claims only partial efficacy. Therefore, only a proportion, perhaps less than half of all travellers' diarrhoea, will be prevented. This may be enough to attract those whose holiday has been spoilt by previous unpleasant episodes. The cholera component will be useful for the handful of travellers who may be at risk, probably not holidaymakers, but healthcare workers going to outbreak areas and refugee camps and backpackers who may be living 'rough'.

● **Typhoid:** this immunisation may be given to those who are travelling to areas where the standards of food and water hygiene are poor. This includes many countries of the tropical and developing world, but if you'll be staying only in first class hotels for a short time (for example, in established resorts in the Caribbean) you may be at very little risk. Being careful about what you eat and drink and your personal hygiene will help to protect you, not only against typhoid, but against all food- and water-borne diseases including travellers' diarrhoea and hepatitis A.

Discuss this with your doctor or travel clinic.

● **Hepatitis A and B:** many people are confused about the types of hepatitis which now stretch along the alphabet from A to G. They are all transmitted either like A or like B. A is passed through infected food and water and B is transmitted like HIV through sexual contact or blood and non-sterile medical equipment.

There are only vaccines against A and B. As hepatitis A is transmitted through food and water, protection is recommended for most of the same areas as typhoid (see pages 20–1). However, hepatitis A is more common than typhoid.

Hepatitis B is transmitted like HIV and so individual behaviour is an important factor. For those who are likely to have sexual contact (heterosexual or homosexual) overseas or who are at extra risk of requiring medical treatment in developing areas, there is a vaccine available. It is not given for most holidays, but usually for longer travel such as backpacking or postings abroad. You can carry condoms from the UK where appropriate, and needle and syringe kits.

Non-routine immunisations

If the type of trip you're taking may pose unusual health risks, or you're going away for a long period or to somewhere very much off the beaten track, other immunisations should be discussed with your doctor. These are not usually given for package holidays – those based in main centres and lasting less than four weeks – although they may be advisable in exceptional circumstances.

● **Rabies:** the risk of rabies is discussed on page 80 and immunisation before departure may be advised if you will be out of reach of medical help or on a long trip through developing areas. It usually causes very little reaction. You must, however, still seek medical help after a bite or scratch from an animal. This may give the impression that the immunisation is not worthwhile but it means that, hopefully, a short delay in reaching modern treatment matters less.

● **Tick-borne encephalitis (TBE):** this vaccine should be considered for walking or camping holidays in wooded areas, or the surrounding countryside, in parts of Europe, especially central and eastern Europe including areas of the former Soviet Union. The risk is more acute in spring and early summer.

Many people going on such holidays do not discover that there may be a risk until they arrive.

An unlicensed vaccine has been available for some years and despite expectations no licensed product

OOOPS!

has arrived. Only having an unlicensed vaccine available has, to some extent, compounded the problem of information reaching those who need it. If you think you may need it, you can ask your travel clinic or family doctor to obtain the vaccine for you.

However, most doctors prefer only to give it if it is likely that the traveller is at some definite risk. It is also relatively expensive. The areas of the Czech Republic, Slovakia, Austria, Hungary, Poland, Germany and Scandinavia affected are quite well mapped, but there is little information about which parts of the former Soviet Union are involved. There are also very small risk areas in other European countries. You should be immunised well in advance of travel if possible, but some protection can be given where time is short.

The disease is transmitted by ticks attaching to people when brushing the undergrowth, so you can discourage them by tucking your trousers into your socks, using insect repellent and checking yourself frequently to remove ticks with tweezers.

● **Meningitis:** there are several different types, including that prevented by the Hib vaccine and the conjugate meningococcal type C vaccine, given to babies routinely. The meningitis vaccine given for travel needs to contain type A, so vaccine containing A and other strains is usually used.

Strain A is rare in the UK, but has caused outbreaks in certain areas of the world, and vaccine is recommended for longer travel especially if you're staying or working with local people or backpacking. Large outbreaks occur in the 'meningitis belt' of Africa. The belt stretches from Senegal in the west to Ethiopia in the east and now extends down the eastern side to Zambia. Package holidays to The Gambia and Kenya are usually considered low risk and immunisation is not routinely given unless an outbreak is reported. Check with your travel clinic before travel.

Proof of immunisation with meningitis vaccine is required for Muslims travelling on the pilgrimage to Mecca in Saudi Arabia (Haj or Umra). No other country requires proof of meningitis immunisation.

Pilgrims on the Haj are required to take the A, C, W, Y vaccine because cases of W meningitis occurred in pilgrims on the Haj of 2000 and 2001. As W meningitis is starting to be reported from Africa, the A, C, W, Y vaccine will tend to be used more.

● **Japanese encephalitis:** this is unlikely to be advised for short package holidays, but it is nowadays needed more often because of the increase in overland trips. It is unlicensed for routine use in the UK, although one type is licensed in the USA. Generally the vaccine is only used for travellers who will spend at least a month staying in rural areas in the endemic zone.

This stretches from parts of India, across south-east Asia to China. There are very few cases in Japan these days. It is spread by mosquitoes which breed in rice fields and bite farm animals, especially pigs. Therefore being out in areas which combine these risk factors (especially after dusk when most of these mosquitoes bite) may make the vaccine worthwhile.

Although your GP can obtain it for you, many family doctors have little experience with it and so may suggest that you get it from a specialist travel clinic. Ideally, you should start the course eight weeks before departure so that three doses can be given over a month, allowing time for it to become effective. However, when time is short, two doses a week apart should provide some protection. On rare occasions, this vaccine has caused allergic reactions so you'd be wise, if you can, to take the last dose at least 10 to 14 days before travelling.

● **Influenza:** this is not usually considered a travel vaccine but those who are in the high-risk groups at home should also be immunised before travel, especially if there will be a group of people travelling together. Outbreaks on cruise ships illustrate the point about group travel. These outbreaks may occur at any time of the year.

● **Special precautions:** anyone who has had their spleen removed may need extra immunisations, and there are special considerations regarding immunisation for pregnant women (see pages 42–5). Some vaccines may not be advisable for those with any serious or chronic disease and in anyone during an infection. Extra vaccines are sometimes recommended for those with chronic disease, for example, pneumococcal vaccine. If you fall into any of these categories, or you are HIV positive, you should discuss with your doctor which immunisations would be sensible, preferably before deciding finally on a destination.

Finally, remember that immunisation cannot give 100 per cent protection against all diseases, and you must follow advice about food and water hygiene and other common-sense guidelines (see later in the book).

MALARIA

Once you have got your immunisations sorted out, you will need to

discuss protection against malaria. You may have seen some of the recent media reports of a vaccine but as yet it is only experimental and does not look likely to become available to travellers in the very near future. It is complicated to make a vaccine against this parasite and at present the trials do not demonstrate adequate protection to make the vaccine useful for holiday travel.

So for the moment, you have to take malaria tablets (strictly speaking, they're antimalarial tablets). Unfortunately they do not provide perfect protection, can be a nuisance to take during your holiday and usually for a month afterwards, and can produce side effects in some people. Therefore it is worth checking carefully whether they are recommended for your chosen destination.

Malaria exists across much of the tropics and malaria maps (see pages 24–5) show many popular holiday countries as endemic zones. However, within these zones there are areas of very low or no risk. As the disease is transmitted by mosquitoes, areas with fewer of them hold less risk. These include mountains, dry areas and deserts, and some cities and main resorts.

There are also tropical areas where the disease has naturally never existed, disappeared or been eradicated, for example, the Caribbean islands (except for Haiti and the Dominican Republic).

If you opt for somewhere with little or no malaria you'll avoid the nuisance of tablet taking and this is a safer bet for anyone who is pregnant or can't take the tablets for some other reason. When checking

FOR A ONE- TO THREE-WEEK HOLIDAY IN HOTEL CONDITIONS.
TRAVEL CLINIC AT THE TIME OF TRAVEL IN CASE OF

For all destinations, check that routine

USA, Canada, Australia, New Zealand, northern and western Europe

- Consider tick-borne encephalitis for certain areas, for example, walking or camping in Austria or southern Sweden, especially in spring and summer
- No malaria

Mediterranean countries including Turkey, North Africa (including Morocco and Tunisia) and eastern Europe

- Consider typhoid, diphtheria/tetanus, hepatitis A and polio, according to conditions expected. In general the risk increases with travel further south and east and outside main hotels and resorts
- Diphtheria up-to-date for countries of the former USSR
- Consider tick-borne encephalitis for parts of eastern Europe, such as areas of the former USSR if camping in spring and summer
- Malaria protection for Turkey (March–November, Antalya eastwards on the south coast and eastern Turkey), and low risk in the summer in some rural areas of Morocco and Armenia, and some southern areas of Azerbaijan, Georgia, Tajikistan and Turkmenistan

The Caribbean including Barbados, St Lucia, Dominican Republic

- Typhoid, diphtheria/tetanus, hepatitis A (typhoid and sometimes hepatitis A less important for stays in first class conditions)
- Malaria protection for Haiti and the Dominican Republic only

THESE GUIDELINES SHOULD BE DISCUSSED WITH YOUR GP OR ANY SPECIAL CIRCUMSTANCES OR RECENT CHANGES.

JK immunisations have been taken.

Tropical South America including Brazil and Venezuela
- Yellow fever (see map, page 13)
- Typhoid, diphtheria/tetanus, hepatitis A
- Malaria protection, especially for the Amazon jungle/forested parts of these countries

West and East Africa including The Gambia, Kenya, Tanzania
- Yellow fever (see map, page 13)
- Typhoid, diphtheria/tetanus, hepatitis A
- Meningitis if outbreaks reported
- Malaria protection

Southern Africa, including South Africa and Zimbabwe
- Typhoid, diphtheria/tetanus, polio, hepatitis A (although less risk in the cities only of South Africa)
- Malaria protection for Zimbabwe and for the game parks and rural north east of South Africa and northern Botswana and Namibia

India and Sri Lanka
- Typhoid, diphtheria/tetanus, polio and hepatitis A
- Malaria protection

For longer, rural, backpacking holidays through developing countries
- Check BCG (TB) and diphtheria
- Consider rabies and hepatitis B
- Consider Japanese encephalitis for parts of India across Asia to China and down through south-east Asia
- Consider meningitis for certain areas (see page 17)
- Malaria protection
  In addition to typhoid, tetanus, polio, hepatitis A and yellow fever (if in yellow fever area)

Vaccine for travel	Number of doses pre-travel
Tetanus **Polio** **Diphtheria**	Usually a single booster (course of three at least 4 weeks apart if no previous course)
Typhoid	One dose vaccine or oral which is three doses
Hepatitis A	One
Yellow fever	One
Meningitis A + C **(meningococcal)** **or A, C, W, Y**	One
Rabies	Three doses over 3–4 weeks
Japanese encephalitis	Three doses over 3 or 4 weeks but two doses at least 1 week apart provide some protection
Tick-borne encephalitis	Two doses 4 weeks apart (reduce to 2 weeks if necessary) or three doses over 3 weeks
Hepatitis B	Two doses 4 weeks apart; third dose 5 months later; see comments
BCG (TB)	One dose only (after skin testing)

Usual minimum interval	Comments (discuss your individual needs with the clinic giving your immunisations)
.0 years	Schoolchildren usually already protected by routine immunisation. Older people may not have had a course. Tetanus no longer available without diphtheria
₃ years (oral – 1 year)	Not usually below 18 months of age. Oral – not below 6 years
Booster 6–12 months later Lasts about 10 years	Not usually given to small children, age varies but not often under 5 years
.0 years	Given at designated centre (some GPs or travel clinics). Not below 9–12 months of age
₅ years	May be less effective below 18 months of age; the travel meningitis is necessary even if the routine meningitis C has been given. A, C, W, Y likely gradually to replace A + C vaccine
₂–3 years	This is the pre-travel schedule (different after a bite, which is still always taken when medical help is reached). Animal handlers always take three doses. Not usually given below 1 year of age
–4 years	Not usually given under 1 year of age. Complete at least 10–14 days before travel
₆–12 months, then 3 years	Not usually given under 1 year of age
–5 years	Third dose can be given 4 weeks after second if necessary, or all three doses within 3 weeks; both these courses are followed by booster at a year. The 3-week course is unsuitable for children
Not usually repeated	Routinely given around age 14 Given in infancy to some high-risk groups

1. CANADA
2. USA
3. MEXICO
4. GUATEMALA
5. BELIZE
6. HONDURAS
7. EL SALVADOR
8. NICARAGUA
9. COSTA RICA
10. CUBA

11. HAITI
12. DOM. REPUBLIC
13. PUERTO RICO
14. PANAMA
15. COLOMBIA
16. VENEZUELA
17. GUYANA
18. SURINAM
19. F. GUIANA
20. ECUADOR
21. PERU
22. BRAZIL
23. BOLIVIA
24. ARGENTINA
25. PARAGUAY
26. URUGUAY
27. CHILE
28. GREENLAND
29. ICELAND
30. NORWAY
31. SWEDEN
32. FINLAND
33. IRISH REP.
34. UK
35. DENMARK
36. GERMANY
37. POLAND
38. FRANCE
39. CZECH REPUBLIC & SLOVAKIA
40. AUSTRIA

41. HUNGARY
42. ROMANIA
43. SPAIN
44. ITALY
45. BOSNIA/CROATIA/SERBIA
46. BULGARIA
47. GREECE
48. PORTUGAL
49. MOROCCO
50. ALGERIA

51. TUNISIA
52. LIBYA
53. W. SAHARA
54. MAURITANIA
55. MALI
56. NIGER
57. CHAD
58. SENEGAL
59. GAMBIA
60. GUINEA BISSA

61. GUINEA
62. BURKINA FASO
63. NIGERIA
64. CAMEROON
65. CEN. AFRICAN REP.
66. SIERRA LEONE
67. LIBERIA
68. IVORY COAST
69. GHANA
70. TOGO

CHECK WITH YOUR GP OR TRAVE

ALARIA TRANSMISSION MAY OCCUR

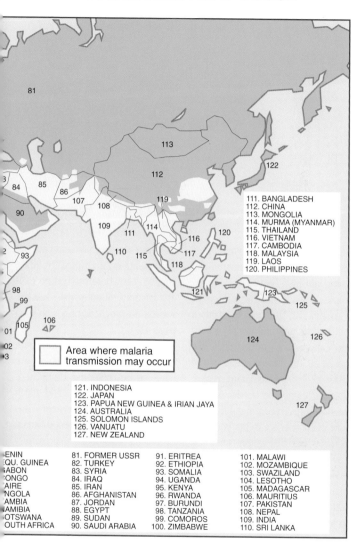

81

113

122

112

84 85 86

107

90 108

109 111 114

110 115

119

116 120

117

118

111. BANGLADESH
112. CHINA
113. MONGOLIA
114. MURMA (MYANMAR)
115. THAILAND
116. VIETNAM
117. CAMBODIA
118. MALAYSIA
119. LAOS
120. PHILIPPINES

93

98
99

106
105

01 102
103

121

123 125

124 126

127

Area where malaria
transmission may occur

121. INDONESIA
122. JAPAN
123. PAPUA NEW GUINEA & IRIAN JAYA
124. AUSTRALIA
125. SOLOMON ISLANDS
126. VANUATU
127. NEW ZEALAND

ENIN	81. FORMER USSR	91. ERITREA	101. MALAWI
QU. GUINEA	82. TURKEY	92. ETHIOPIA	102. MOZAMBIQUE
ABON	83. SYRIA	93. SOMALIA	103. SWAZILAND
ONGO	84. IRAQ	94. UGANDA	104. LESOTHO
AIRE	85. IRAN	95. KENYA	105. MADAGASCAR
NGOLA	86. AFGHANISTAN	96. RWANDA	106. MAURITIUS
AMBIA	87. JORDAN	97. BURUNDI	107. PAKISTAN
AMIBIA	88. EGYPT	98. TANZANIA	108. NEPAL
OTSWANA	89. SUDAN	99. COMOROS	109. INDIA
OUTH AFRICA	90. SAUDI ARABIA	100. ZIMBABWE	110. SRI LANKA

_INIC FOR THE UP-TO-DATE SITUATION

TABLETS FOR PREVENTION OF MALARIA

Proper name	Common trade names	Interval
Chloroquine	Avloclor	Weekly
	Nivaquine	Weekly
Proguanil	Paludrine	Daily
Mefloquine	Lariam	Weekly
Doxycycline	Vibramycin	Daily
Atovaquone and proguanil	Malarone	Daily

whether malaria is present, it is necessary to consider the area and resort, not just the country. For example, Thailand has two categories of malaria risk, the most resistant on the borders with Burma (Myanmar) and Cambodia and conversely low risk in all the tourist areas of the south except for Ko Chang Island, near the Cambodia border. Tablets are no longer recommended apart from the border areas, but you have to remember that a very small risk may still exist.

That means that if by any chance you feel ill with a temperature after you get back, right up to about a year later, you should remind your doctor that you've been to a possible malaria area so that the condition can be ruled out as a cause of your symptoms or treated if necessary.

If you are pregnant and have set your heart on a tropical holiday, choose one where there is no malaria or only minimal risk (see the section on pregnancy beginning on page 42).

When you're going somewhere where malaria is a risk, tablets are likely to be recommended. There are a few areas of the world which are not considered 'resistant'. This means that the more serious strain of malaria (Plasmodium falciparum) is not resistant to the ordinary malaria drug chloroquine (and, increasingly, other drugs too). However, these zones are shrinking all the time as resistance spreads and the only areas where chloroquine alone can be used for prevention are parts of Central America, North Africa and the Middle East, including Turkey.

Chloroquine is available without a prescription. The two common trade names by which it is usually known are in the table above.

When resistance creeps in, either another drug is given with the chloroquine – usually proguanil (known by its trade name Paludrine) – or a quite separate drug is used.

Several once-weekly malaria tablets have been tried as an alternative to taking a combination of proguanil and chloroquine. As this combination consists of a total of 16 tablets each week, the attraction of a single tablet is obvious. The problem has been that there is no perfect tablet to meet this requirement. The once-weekly 'wonder drug' mefloquine (Lariam), greeted enthusiastically about ten years ago, also has side effects in some people. There are, however, few truly effective drugs which do not produce unwanted reactions in some people and mefloquine is valuable because of its effectiveness for travellers to highly resistant, high transmission areas such as much of Africa. There is now a choice of two other tablets so no one has to take mefloquine; however, where it is considered the best tablet the doctor should check your medical history carefully before prescribing it. More side effects have been reported than in other countries. It is important that these are monitored carefully, and the more serious ones separated from the minor.

The more common complaints include vivid dreams and feeling lightheaded (which tend to settle gradually) and nausea which is reduced if the tablet is taken after the evening meal with water.

The serious concerns include

reports of mood change which may go on to depression, anxiety or hallucinations or even very rare reports of fits. While these are obviously alarming, it's important to remember that the majority of people do not experience such problems, and it could be unwise to deny travellers to high-risk areas the option of one of the highest protection tablets. The two other drugs that are an alternative to mefloquine are doxycycline and malarone. Proguanil and chloroquine are still retained for certain areas such as the Indian subcontinent. You should always get up-to-date advice from your GP or travel clinic on individual choice of tablet and action to take if side effects occur.

Proguanil and chloroquine are not without side effects either. They are well known for producing gastrointestinal problems from nausea to diarrhoea. These can be dramatically reduced by taking the tablets after the evening meal. There are few serious adverse effects, although mouth ulcers can be unpleasant and hair thinning worries some people. The hair problem usually only arises on longer trips rather than on an average length holiday. Hair growth usually returns to normal after the end of the course.

Doxycycline, an antibiotic, is increasingly being used as an alternative to mefloquine. This is taken daily and like all malaria tablets has advantages and disadvantages. The main advantage as perceived by most travellers is that it does not appear to produce the neuropsychiatric effects that follow mefloquine use in a minority of people.

However, its main downside is that a small proportion (probably about one per cent) of people become allergic to sunlight so that their skin burns more easily. This can mean that they have to stop the doxycycline and seek other forms of protection. Obviously, a high-factor sunscreen is advised to reduce the chance of the reaction. Some women are more prone to thrush while on doxycycline (normally readily treatable); it can make the birth control pill less effective and, although it often prevents travellers' diarrhoea, it can occasionally cause severe diarrhoea.

Having said this, the side effects are suffered by a minority and are usually felt to be worth the risk to obtain a good level of malarial protection.

The other alternative to Lariam is a new tablet, Malarone, which was licensed in 2001. It is a very welcome addition to the range of antimalarials. It is a combination of proguanil and atovaquone, the former being one of the well-established antimalarials and the latter a drug used in the treatment of unusual pneumonias. Malarone, although expensive, has the great advantage of being taken for just one week after leaving the malarial area (all the others need to be taken for four weeks afterwards).

Malarone appears to have neither the psychiatric side effects nor the side effects of doxycycline. As with all of the choices, it can cause gastric symptoms and should be taken after a main meal to reduce them. Until it has been in use for several years, the full picture will not be known, but the signs point towards a very useful and effective drug. Its major use to date has been for short trips (usually less than four weeks) to higher-risk areas.

Malarone has recently been licensed for use in children; however, doxycycline is not suitable for children under 12 years – a reminder that the choice of antimalarials for children is not as wide as in adults and of the unsuitability of choosing high-risk malarial areas for family holidays.

Proguanil and chloroquine are the only antimalarial pills that are available over the counter. Chloroquine should not generally be taken by people with epilepsy, and it may make psoriasis worse, although this is uncommon in those with mild psoriasis. Proguanil may not be suitable for anyone who takes drugs (except aspirin) to reduce blood clotting.

Taking malaria tablets both during the holiday and for four weeks afterwards is hard enough for adults, but it is even more difficult to persuade children to do it. It is far easier to plan to avoid malarial areas if at all possible. There are no children's syrups available as alternatives to the majority of malaria tablets. Doses of medication must be checked carefully with the doctor, nurse or pharmacist, as they may vary from those on the packet.

It is obvious from these descriptions that there are no easy answers when it comes to malaria tablets. However, there are some very important points to bear in mind:

- No tablet provides complete protection against malaria
- Take positive steps to reduce the number of mosquito bites, particularly after dusk
- Get current advice on choice of malaria tablets for you and your holiday
- Remember to continue the tablets for four weeks after leaving the last malarial area (or one week for Malarone)
- Forgetting to take the tablets causes as many problems as drug resistance
- Report any possible symptoms to a doctor for diagnosis and treatment.

With the growth of off-the-beaten-track holidays, there are a few situations where people may need to carry emergency drug therapy against malaria (available only on prescription).

It is always better to obtain competent medical treatment, but there are shortages of medicines in some rural areas and you may need to offer yours to the doctor for use in treating you. The drugs are not supplied with the idea of self-treatment except where there is no medical help at all.

As no tablet provides complete protection, you have to use other means of reducing the risk as well. Malaria is transmitted by the bite of the anopheles mosquito (females only, the males are vegetarian!). The female bites between dusk and dawn so that is the most important

time to protect yourself against getting bitten.

One way is to put on cover-up clothes before dusk, that is, wear long sleeves and long trousers or a long skirt. Of course this won't be completely effective. Small mosquitoes may manage to get inside loose clothes and larger ones may bite through the material, but it should reduce the frequency. When there are mosquitoes about apply insect repellent to exposed skin.

There has been a lot of discussion about types of repellent, but the most widely used and effective ingredient is diethyltoluamide (DEET). It has been used on the skin of such massive numbers of people world wide, it would be surprising if there had not been rare reports of toxicity possibly associated with it. As a result of

this you must take care not to exceed the manufacturers' instructions about applying it, especially for children.

Naturally care should be taken to avoid the eyes. A skin patch test may be a wise precaution for people with sensitive skins. Spray or roll-on formulations avoid spills of repellents which can mark plastics, including cameras, and reduces the chance of a child trying to drink them.

For those who cannot use DEET, there is a range of other repellent products containing various essential oils. In most cases they do not have quite the same effect. People often ask about the use of vitamin B or garlic pills as insect repellents. They may be effective for some individuals, but when tested, no consistent protection is demonstrated. There is no doubt that differences in skin excretions make some people more attractive to mosquitoes than others.

Some repellents can be sprayed on to clothing, although some may make a slight mark. This can be useful around collars and trouser legs, and can reduce the amount applied directly on to the skin. Recently, there have been insecticide sprays developed that are designed for spraying on clothes.

You also need to prevent bites while you are in bed at night. Most international hotels have modern air-conditioning systems which discourage mosquitoes. However, they could fly in if someone leaves a door or window open and then you would need to use knock-down insect (fly) killer to spray the room after closing the door and windows. Where you need to sleep with the windows open (because there is no air conditioning) there should be screens on the windows and, in high-risk areas, a mosquito net provided over the beds. Nets are more effective when they are dipped in an insecticide called permethrin. Anyone who has to carry their own net, for example, backpacking off the beaten track, should be aware of this.

Smoke coils are burnt to discourage insects in many tropical countries and may be useful when sitting on a veranda. However, they will not burn reliably all night so there is a better alternative to use if there are electrical sockets in your room: a small plug-in device which vaporises a tablet of insecticide placed on it. You will need to remember to carry an international adapter as well.

Besides malaria mosquitoes, there are other insects that transmit disease: sandflies, ticks and other mosquitoes, for example, those that carry Dengue fever (not usually as serious as malaria, but certainly very unpleasant). Dengue is on the increase in the Caribbean, Central and South America, and most of

Asia. It also exists in a few Pacific Islands and in tropical Queensland. There is no specific prevention or treatment apart from reducing mosquito bites. Mosquitoes can also be a real nuisance, but not usually dangerous, in many northern holiday destinations such as Canada, Alaska and Scandinavia. The same information on repellents and cover-up clothes applies, but it should be remembered that a lot of insects are daytime biters so the precautions do not only apply to after dark.

FIRST AID KIT

Different people and destinations have different requirements, so treat the lists on pages 32–3 as a guideline. You'll only need a basic selection for a short holiday to a major destination. It's worth discussing any queries with your doctor or pharmacist and make sure you read the packet information supplied with all medications.

Consult your doctor about the suitability of antibiotics for travel away from medical help.

You may also want to have a dental check-up, especially before holidays in developing areas.

FIRST AID KIT FOR ADULTS

Medication
- Antiseptic, dressings and plasters
- Paracetamol or other mild painkiller
- Antacid indigestion remedy
- Dry throat lozenges
- Insect repellent
- Calamine lotion
- Cream to relieve insect bites
- Antihistamine tablets
- Motion sickness tablets
- Diarrhoea 'stopper' tablets, for example, loperamide
- Oral rehydration salts
- Laxative
- Athlete's foot powder } If you're prone to
- Vaginal thrush treatment } suffer and for travel
- Anti-malarial pills where necessary } in hot countries
- Supply of any regular medication(s)
- Consider antibiotic for general use or travellers' diarrhoea if likely to be away from medical help

Equipment
- Thermometer
- Tweezers
- Scissors
- Ear plugs
- Sunscreen
- Lipsalve
- Contact lens solution
- Spare spectacles or prescription
- Water purifying tablets
- Sterile needles and syringe kit
- Condoms
- Tampons

FIRST AID KIT FOR CHILDREN

Check the package for suitability and dosage for age of child.
If in doubt ask the pharmacist or your GP.

Medication

- Children's paracetamol
- Oral rehydration salts
- Calamine lotion
- Antiseptic, dressings and plasters
- Insect repellent
- Anti-malaria tablets/syrup
- Motion sickness preparation } where
- Supply of any regular medication(s) } necessary

- Nappy rash cream } for
- Teething gel } appropriate
- Plenty of baby wipes } ages

Equipment

- High factor sunscreen
- Thermometer for children, e.g. forehead strips
- Tweezers
- Sterilising equipment for babies' bottles
- Wet tissues
- Equipment to boil water (and allow to cool) for drinking
  (where necessary)

KEY POINTS

✓ Consider any health risk before you choose your holiday destination

✓ Even when no mandatory immunisations are required, take medical advice on health precautions

✓ Try to plan your immunisations early, but remember that some useful protection can be obtained even at short notice

✓ Obtain medical advice on choice of malaria tablets, but remember that no tablets provide total protection, so reduce mosquito bites as far as possible and seek medical help if you are ill during or after a visit to a malarial area

✓ Travel medical insurance is very important (always check the small print)

Women and children only

TRAVELLING WITH CHILDREN

It's worth doing a bit of advance planning and preparation to make the holiday more enjoyable for everyone. Usually, before you go, take the opportunity to check that the childhood immunisation schedule has been completed and enquire about whether your child needs any further immunisations.

It can be difficult getting malaria tablets into babies and small children and there are no children's formulations of most varieties. It is often a matter of breaking tablets and persuading the child to take repeated doses of bitter tablets while you're away and for four weeks after your return. It can easily turn into a battle of wills, so you might be wiser to opt for holidays

outside malarial areas for the time being at least.

Try to book your airline seat well in advance for longer journeys with a young baby to make sure a 'sky cot' is available. Babies can suck a bottle and children can suck a sweet on take off and landing to help them equalise pressure in their ears which otherwise is uncomfortable. Crying has the same effect. 'Blocked' ears due to infection should be medically checked before travel and sometimes flying may have to be delayed.

Motion sickness is rare in very small children but common between three and twelve years of age. A vomit bag may be a sensible precaution and the chemist can provide mild medication for those known to suffer. Being able to see the view outside to the horizon might help. Reading or doing puzzles may not. Don't forget to pack toys or amusements for the journey in your hand baggage, bearing in mind that there'll probably be limited play space.

Simple medicaments should also be in your hand luggage and so available at all stages of the journey. Children's painkillers, nappies, antiseptic creams, a few plasters plus the oral rehydration salts and a children's thermometer need to be included, together with supplies of any regular medication taken already by your child. You might like to discuss with your doctor whether to carry a mild paediatric sedative to have in reserve for an exceptionally long journey.

Wet or antiseptic tissues for cleaning their hands after the lavatory and before handling food are also useful.

Pack suitable clothes in your hand luggage, bearing in mind any likely changes in temperature between home and your final destination. When packing for hot climates, do not take only short sleeved clothes but remember that you'll probably need to be able to cover your child's arms, legs and head against the sun (and sometimes to reduce the area of skin exposed to insect bites).

You'll need to allow for unforeseen delays on the journey when packing supplies of suitable food and drink. If possible check the availability of baby foods at your destination particularly in tropical or developing countries. Bought milk can be a source of infection and breast-feeding has obvious advantages. If you are breast-feeding, you must be sure to drink adequate quantities of water yourself in hot climates. Children can dehydrate quickly and especially if they develop diarrhoea or vomiting.

Plenty of safe drinks should always be available and you should take packets of oral rehydration salts which can be mixed with boiled or bottled water. These help to restore the balance of salts and help the body to retain fluids. They must be reconstituted exactly according to the manufacturer's instructions (particularly for babies) so don't be tempted to make them up any stronger. Small children shouldn't take tablets designed to stop diarrhoea, so food and water hygiene is especially important for the very young. Always seek medical attention earlier rather than later for young children with diarrhoea, particularly if they have a temperature.

Don't use too much insect repellent or apply it too frequently to young children's skin – in other words, don't exceed the quantities recommended on the pack. You shouldn't put it on their hands either as they may then rub it into their eyes or mouth. Spraying it directly on to collars, cuffs and trouser legs will cut down the amount you need to apply to their skin.

Where insects are a real problem and you've had to put repellent on all exposed areas of skin, wash it off once you go indoors.

You will have to make an effort to ration the amount of time children spend out in hot sun, and always use a high protection factor sunscreen for them.

Accidents can happen in new environments and you'll need to take particular care close to the sea or swimming pool. Children have disappeared or been drowned when their parents have been distracted for only a few minutes. Any animal bite or scratch must be seen by a doctor in a country where rabies exists. This should be done especially quickly for any injury to the face or head which is more likely where children rather than adults are concerned.

As always, medical insurance is important for overseas travel and children may be included free.

WOMEN ON HOLIDAY

Women may have more concerns about the standards of hygiene and lavatories they are likely to encounter on holiday, especially in developing countries and away from the major holiday centres. As a woman, you may also have

specific queries, for example, about travel and the contraceptive pill and about personal safety concerns.

In places where washing your hands properly may not always be practical, it is worth carrying some packs of moist tissues. Your hands need to be clean before you insert a tampon as well as after using the lavatory. A roll of loo paper may be useful in countries with different customs such as India. It may not be available except in major westernised hotels. Tampons are not available in many developing countries apart from main tourist centres.

For camping, sailing or other situations where you might prefer to postpone a menstrual period, your GP or family planning clinic can often prescribe the contraceptive pill or suggest how you could adapt the way you take your present one. Should you have a gastrointestinal upset causing you to vomit a few (probably up to three or four) hours after taking a pill, you can take another one.

With travellers' diarrhoea it is more difficult to estimate how much protection has been lost. You should keep on taking your pill, but also use an additional form of contraception such as a condom because you cannot rely on the pill again until the next cycle.

The same applies if you're taking some types of antibiotic, except that the extra precautions are advisable for 14 days after the course. One malaria tablet called doxycycline may make the pill less effective for the first month you are taking doxycycline. Before travelling, it is wise to check current advice in these situations for your individual contraceptive pill. As missed pills can cause problems, always pack them in your hand luggage.

A new contraceptive patch applied once weekly will avoid the problems of the pill being less effective as a result of travellers' diarrhoea or antibiotics/malaria tablets. It could be a very convenient method of contraception for women travellers. Another method of avoiding daily pills is to arrange for depo injected contraception from your GP or family planning clinic. However, this method would be unsuitable for use just before travel because it is not reversible in the case of side effects. It should be tried out well in advance of departure. An implant (Implanon) lasting several years could be attractive for long-term travellers. It can, if necessary, be removed, but only by a doctor trained in the technique. Another point about contraceptive hormones and hormone replacement therapy (HRT) is that the small risk of deep vein thrombosis (DVT) with these products may be increased by long-haul flights (see section on DVT, page 55).

Some women find their periods stop on longer trips and this can be quite convenient so long as you have no reason to think that you might be pregnant. Some women

may like to carry condoms which also help to prevent sexually transmitted diseases – in some countries it can be difficult for women to buy condoms. In an emergency you can ask a doctor to prescribe the 'morning after' pill, which you can take up to 72 hours after unprotected intercourse. In the UK this pill is available over the counter from a chemist.

Thrush is more common in hot climates because the yeast organism which causes it multiplies faster in warm, humid conditions. Your genital area should be kept clean, avoiding irritation by soap. Cotton underclothes are a good idea but tight trousers aren't as they prevent circulation of air. If you know you're prone to thrush, especially if on doxycycline anti-malarial tablets you may find it useful to carry some clotrimazole or econazole which you can buy from the chemist or get on prescription from your doctor. Even more convenient is the 'over-the counter', single capsule, fluconazole.

Urine infections can also be common in hot climates especially in those who are prone to them at home. They can be very inconvenient as you feel you have to pass urine more often and, when you do, there is a burning sensation.

Drinking plenty of fluids, especially in hot climates, is worthwhile, both as a preventive and also because it helps to relieve symptoms once they have occurred. The burning may be relieved by taking potassium citrate, available from the chemist.

Cranberry juice is a popular remedy in the USA and it is widely available in supermarkets. If the symptoms do not settle, and particularly if you have a temperature or back pain, then you should see a doctor as antibiotics may be needed.

Women travelling alone may encounter more problems than men in the same situation, although the risk of being attacked exists for either sex. No written advice can replace common sense and caution. Planning the journey so that hitch-hiking and long waits in bus or train stations are unnecessary is a sensible precaution.

Always make sure someone knows your expected itinerary and times of arrival. Obviously keep cameras and valuables out of sight and dress modestly. This is particularly important in Muslim countries where exposing a lot of female skin or wearing tight, figure-hugging clothes can be equated with loose morals. The same judgement may be made of women travelling without a male 'protector'. It may be necessary to cover your head and/or arms to visit holy places in various countries. The Foreign and Commonwealth Office (FCO) website and telephone line provide advice on security and some local customs in individual countries.

TRAVEL IN PREGNANCY

Pregnant women often want to have a holiday before their lives become more restricted by the arrival of a baby. Many enjoy travelling and suffer no

problems; however, there is no doubt that if something goes wrong, most would have preferred to be at home.

Your choice of destination and time of travel can be important, so it is wise to think carefully and perhaps discuss the possibilities with your doctor before booking your holiday. Try to find out about the likely standard of medical facilities in the destination country. Malarial areas should be avoided because, although some tablets can be taken in pregnancy if necessary, it is not an ideal situation. Most women would prefer not to take medication during pregnancy and no tablets can provide complete protection. Malaria is more serious in pregnancy.

It is also ideal to avoid immunisations, although again, if the risk of disease is high enough, some may be given. It is preferable not to be put into that position, so choose somewhere outside the yellow fever belt (Africa and the north part of South America – see maps on pages 13–14) and away from the areas of higher risk from food- and water-borne diseases. Be prepared to stay in hotels where the catering hygiene standards are likely to be relatively high or where you can cater for yourself and take special care.

The most common time for a miscarriage to happen is at around 12 weeks and some women need a minor operation if it is not complete. This is straightforward with modern medical facilities, but would not be ideal in a developing country. Morning sickness and nausea are also usually more of a problem early in pregnancy. In the last three months, the possibility of early

MALARIA – BETTER SAFE. . .

If you can, opt for the less risky areas, and you'll have a more relaxing holiday

SAFEST DESTINATIONS WHEN PREGNANT
(i.e. good medical treatment available)
- Europe (except eastern)
- USA and Canada (but expensive if you need treatment)
- Australia and New Zealand (but a long way from home)

EXAMPLES OF TROPICAL CLIMATES WITH LITTLE OR NO MALARIA RISK
- Caribbean islands (except Haiti and the Dominican Republic)
- Singapore
- Penang and most of peninsular Malaysia
- Seychelles
- Bangkok, Pattaya, Phuket (Thailand)
- Queensland (Australia)
- Florida, Hawaii (USA)

HIGH RISK OF MALARIA (AVOID IF POSSIBLE WHEN PREGNANT)
- East, West and Central Africa
- Amazon basin areas of South America
- Burma (Myanmar)
- Vietnam
- Cambodia and Laos
- Sabah
- Papua New Guinea, Vanuatu, Solomon Islands
- Rural far south China (Yunnan and Hainan provinces)
- Northern and border areas of Thailand

ALWAYS CHECK THE UP-TO-DATE SITUATION WITH YOUR DOCTOR OR A TRAVEL CLINIC

delivery means you should be close to high standards of medical help. By this stage anyway, your size and general discomfort may also make long journeys and holidays in a hot climate uncomfortable. Airlines may refuse to carry pregnant women after 36 weeks.

This leaves the middle three months (especially 18 to 24 weeks) as the best choice for those who want to get away. Check your airline's policy with regard to pregnancy and read the small print on your travel insurance.

When making your plans, remember that pregnancy can increase fatigue, hunger and how often your bladder needs to be emptied. Your ankles can swell more during flights and hours of travel can leave you with backache, so try and allow for all this when planning your schedule. In any case it is important to try to move around during the flight and consider the use of travel socks to reduce the risk of DVT, which can be higher in pregnancy.

KEY POINTS

✓ Plan your destination carefully, checking local facilities

✓ Avoid malarial areas in pregnancy and when travelling with small children

✓ Keep essential supplies for your baby close to hand

✓ Don't delay seeking medical help if a young child develops diarrhoea, especially if accompanied by a fever

✓ Women travellers should be particularly aware of personal safety

In good health?

WHEN YOU'RE OLDER

Many older people are taking holidays away from home whether in the UK or in places much further afield such as Canada or Australia where many have family. The majority have no problems at all, but it is worth spending a little time beforehand to consider any potential difficulties and how to overcome or get round them.

Before you book, there are a number of points worth considering.

- Will you have any difficulty coping with the rigours of a long-haul flight and the distances that have to be walked at some major airports?
- How will you deal with any large time change?

- Will there be a dramatic temperature difference between home and your destination?
- Pre-existing health conditions are one of the most common reasons for significant health problems abroad.
- What are medical services like where you're going?
- Travel insurance can sometimes be more expensive for those over 65 or over 70. Check that you will be covered by paying the basic premium or whether there's an additional charge. The same applies to those with any pre-existing health condition. Many insurance companies will not provide cover even for an extra premium. Specialist companies may need to be contacted. Always read the small print.

There is an Age Concern Insurance Service which offers holiday insurance. You can get more information by telephoning Age Concern (see 'Useful information' on page 101).

When you've travelled a long way, you may well want to make the most of it by touring around to see as much of the country as possible. Remember to allow yourself enough time to recover from the long distance flight before arranging any rigorous excursions.

There are societies that provide newsletters and discount flights for those with relatives abroad. Two are mentioned in the Age Concern fact sheet 'Holidays for Older People', which also lists commercial organisations that offer special holidays for older people. It also gives useful information about arranging for pension payments if you're going to be away for some time.

Whatever your age, you must remember to pack any medicines in your hand baggage rather than in your suitcase. Just in case you should lose them, carry a separate letter giving the generic (proper) rather than the trade names of any medicines you take, plus a doctor's letter if you have any condition which might mean you need medical attention while you're away.

A spare pair of spectacles or a prescription could also be a wise precaution.

Those born before 1960 should allow longer for travel vaccines where possible (see page 8). The increase in numbers of older people travelling in recent years is also producing an increase in the number of travellers with pre-existing health conditions such as cardiac or respiratory diseases. Younger people with chronic conditions, for example, epilepsy or HIV, also wish to travel to more adventurous destinations. In all these cases an assessment needs to be made of their fitness to travel and the availability and suitability of medical treatment at the destination, should it become necessary. Extra precautions for these people may include additional immunisations, different malaria tablets, advice to carry antibiotics, arrangements with the airline for the use of supplementary oxygen during the flight or assisted transportation at the airport. After careful consideration of the health needs of some individuals, certain destinations may be unsuitable. These decisions should be taken before, and not after, the holiday is booked.

IF YOU HAVE DIABETES

In addition to the plans that everyone makes before going away, you may need to take some extra precautions to avoid potential problems.

Tablet treatment

You may like to talk to your doctor or diabetes nurse about any adjustments to the timing of doses if you're going on a very long flight, but most people will have no problems. You may not be aware that some types of tablet can increase the risk of sunburn in some individuals, so take extra care in the sun. When you're going somewhere hot, pack some cover-up clothes and plenty of sunblock. Carry your tablets on your person or in your hand baggage.

Insulin treatment

If you don't already do so, consider

wearing some sort of identification bracelet in case you are unable to let other people know in an emergency that you have diabetes. Bracelets are available from MedicAlert, or from SOS Talisman Co. Ltd (see 'Useful information' pages 104–5). Again, if you don't have one already, it's worth carrying a wallet identification card with your photo which verifies your need to carry syringes and medical equipment. It has no legal status but could be helpful at customs and is translated into French, Greek, German and Spanish. Identity cards are available from Diabetes UK (see 'Useful information' on page 102).

A doctor's letter or clinic card with type and dosage of insulin and any other special information is always a wise precaution. Of course insulin must be kept easily available en route with needles and syringes, blood glucose testing strips, glucose tablets or other quick snack food (like biscuits) in case of hypo attacks or delayed meals.

Planning your insulin requirements for crossing time zones needs consideration for long eastward or westward flights, and you should discuss your individual needs in advance with your doctor or diabetes nurse. Some people prefer to keep a watch set, and thus their insulin programme, on home time until after arrival and then adjust gradually by two or three hours at a time. Others prefer to adjust using a pen system with soluble (fast-acting) insulin which is very flexible and can be adapted to the journey. The key is to monitor your blood glucose levels both before and after the flight, and for long journeys two or three times on the plane.

Probably the best way to transport your insulin is in a polystyrene container or a wide-necked vacuum flask which has been cooled in advance by rinsing out with cold water. This will do for most journeys if kept out of direct sunlight. If it can be refrigerated during a long journey, that is ideal, but do not allow it to be frozen (for example, in an aircraft luggage hold). Think about taking a needle clipper to help with disposal.

You'll need to take extra care to avoid diarrhoea and vomiting by paying special attention to food and water hygiene and washing your hands frequently. If you do have a bout of gastroenteritis, your insulin requirements will need careful monitoring and you should seek medical help in good time. Insulin requirements may alter in hot climates, which is another reason for frequent monitoring. It is also worth taking trouble to protect your feet during unaccustomed walking in sandals or shoes in hot climates. Fungal or other foot infections or injuries should be treated promptly.

Find out in advance about medical facilities in the country you're visiting.

Diabetes UK produce travel guides for about 60 countries cheaply, along with a lot of other useful literature. There are also insurance brokers who could be especially useful if the standard policies on offer exclude pre-existing disease.

Travelling with a companion who understands about your diabetes can be reassuring.

IF YOU HAVE A DISABILITY

Again, careful pre-planning with the airline and with your choice of destination and hotel will make the holiday much more successful. Anyone who uses a wheelchair ideally needs one that is lightweight, foldable and as narrow as possible, as well as being robust and easily repairable. A strong person to push the chair may be preferable to a chair that's battery operated.

USEFUL ADDRESSES FOR DISABLED PEOPLE

More details about these organisations can be found in 'Useful addresses' on page 101.

RADAR (Royal Association for Disability and Rehabilitation; tel: 020 7250 3222) produces information sheets and two handbooks *Getting There* and *Holidays in Britain and Ireland*

The Disabled Living Foundation (0845 130 9177) can provide advice on equipment for the disabled traveller

Tripscope (08457 585641) is a charity that can also advise on transport and arrange escorts

Holiday Care (0845 124 9971) is a charity that provides information on hotels and visitor attractions in the UK accessible to people with disabilities and their carers. Publishes information sheets on overseas destinations.

The British Red Cross Society (020 7235 5454) loans out equipment such as wheelchairs, commodes and bedpans

John Grooms (08456 584478) has information on holidays in the UK and hotel facilities in London

The Winged Fellowship Trust (020 7833 2594) runs holiday homes for people with disabilities

The Automobile Association Disability Helpline (0800 262050) produces a publication, *The Disabled Travellers' Guide*, free to AA members

KEY POINTS

✓ Choose a destination and itinerary realistically suitable for your abilities

✓ Check the local medical facilities at your destination

✓ If you have any health problems, it is wise to: check with your doctor about fitness to fly; and enquire from the airline about assistance at the airport or any requirements for a medical form

✓ Check that there are no exclusions in your travel medical insurance

✓ People with diabetes need specialist advice about carrying insulin and especially if travelling over many time zones

JET LAG

Anyone who's making a long journey, especially east or west, may worry that the beginning of their trip will be spoiled by the effects of jet lag. It is caused by crossing several time zones going east or west from home. People disagree about whether travelling east or west causes the worst symptoms. Most people, but not all, prefer to travel west. This is supposed to be because the natural body rhythm settles to a slightly longer day once it is not bound by light and darkness.

Travelling directly southwards down Africa may cause fatigue from hours of travelling but involves less of the time change element that compounds the symptoms of east–west travel. Crossing time zones in a jet aircraft can land you many hours ahead of or behind home time. The fatigue of travelling is exacerbated by lost sleep plus the body's natural rhythms being upset. No one feels like getting up at 3am and eating a large meal because that is usually rest time. It takes six days or sometimes even longer for these circadian rhythms to adapt fully, although you may feel better long before.

From time to time there are new 'jet lag diets' published, or new 'cures' which involve everything from complicated changes in sleep and meal times before travel to aromatherapy.

The truth is that none of these works completely, but an understanding of the problem can reduce the suffering.

Adopting local bed and meal times helps adaptation. For long flights, it may be worth trying to book one which arrives in the early evening, so you have time to get to your hotel and then stretch your legs or take some easy relaxation shortly before bed. However, most of us choose holiday flights on the basis of dates or price rather than exact arrival time and so this may not be practical. In fact, if you arrive at your holiday destination feeling tired, this shouldn't matter much, and isn't really worth worrying about, although the same may not apply on a business trip. Try to allow for taking things easy

in the first few days, and don't let it bother you if you need to rest a fair bit – you're on holiday after all!

If you're very keen to adapt quickly, try moving your meal (and even sleep) times nearer towards those of the arrival time zone before you set off. However, by doing this, you may only shift some of the inconvenience back to home instead of experiencing it on arrival.

It is useful to reduce your sleep deprivation as much as you can. Sleeping or resting as much as possible on a long flight will help. Many travellers opt for the 'natural' sleep-inducing or relaxing effect of small amounts of alcohol when flying. However, long flights are dehydrating, and alcohol or strong coffee can add to the effect. Water, lots of it, makes you feel better, especially if you've been drinking alcohol. Nowadays, it is considered better not to take anything that encourages sleeping slumped in one position because of the risk (small) of deep vein thrombosis (see below), so a balance between rest and moving about the cabin is necessary.

Melatonin, a new so-called 'cure', is available outside the UK. It is a pineal gland hormone which is naturally secreted in the evening. Bright light inhibits its production.

It appears that melatonin taken before sleep is needed works well for many people overseas who have already used it. However, further research evaluation of any long-term effects is required before it can be medically recommended.

As light naturally inhibits melatonin production, going out into sunshine or bright artificial light does seem to aid alertness. Again more research is needed into the timings and quantities of light required.

Eating protein-rich meals (which are high in a chemical called tyrosine) at breakfast and lunch may help an active day. In the evening, eating a meal with carbohydrates provides tryptophan to help natural production of the hormones necessary for sleep. Such measures often fit easily into holiday plans and may help adaptation.

The most important point is not to get too worked up about the potential for jet lag on a holiday. It may be pleasant to relax with aromatherapy or other relaxing therapies offered by the hotel on arrival and to allow your body to adapt gently. People vary enormously in their rates of adaptation. Those who really find jet lag a major problem would do better to choose holidays with short air journeys if they're going east or west, although long flights south should pose fewer problems. If you've set your heart on far east or west travel, you could consider the possibility of going by sea and road or accept that you'll need lots of time to acclimatise if you do fly.

DEEP VEIN THROMBOSIS

Sitting in restricted conditions for many hours predisposes to deep vein thrombosis (DVT), just as lying immobile in a hospital bed has been recognised to cause DVT. Long distance journeys by road, as well as longer flights, have been implicated. The blood clot (which is what the DVT is) in the calf of the leg can become dangerous if particles of the clot reach the lungs; deaths have been reported, although rarely.

Although DVT in travellers is a rare condition, certain people who have the following conditions may be at slightly higher risk. These include pregnancy, those on oestrogen-containing contraceptive or HRT, obesity, some individuals with congestive heart failure, older age groups, blood disorders which increase clotting risk, previous clot, malignancy and recent surgery, especially of the abdomen and lower limbs.

Travellers can take various precautions to reduce the risk, including moving about the cabin where practicable and exercising the calf muscles while seated, so increasing the rate of blood circulation in the lower legs and discouraging pooling of blood.

Travel socks help to fulfil the same function. Keeping well hydrated by drinking lots of soft drinks may possibly reduce risk and certainly makes you feel better. Some people who have no bleeding tendencies, ulcers or other contraindications to aspirin like to take one on the day of a long-haul flight; however, aspirin is more effective at reducing the risk of clots in arteries than in veins. The risk accumulates for those people with more than one factor and, therefore, it is sensible to seek advice from your doctor before travel. A few travellers will be advised to take anticoagulant therapy.

SAFE SUN

There has been a lot of publicity recently about the dangers of sunlight even in the UK. The skin cancer rate has risen by about eight per cent annually in recent years and increased exposure to sunlight has been implicated as one cause. Obviously the sun is much stronger in the Mediterranean and even more so in the tropics, and while no one wants to stop you enjoying the sun, you do need to take care (although some dermatologists would warn that any suntan is a sign of skin damage).

- Limit the amount of time you spend out in the sun, especially at first and around the middle of the day.
- Choose cover-up clothes and get everyone to wear a broad-brimmed hat. This is particularly important if your skin is the type that burns easily and for babies and children. It appears

that sunburn under age 15 years may be an important risk factor for skin cancer later on. For people with brown or black skin the risk of sun-induced skin cancer is minimal.

- Choose a sunscreen which filters out both UVA and UVB rays. The sun protection factor (SPF) number on the packaging gives an indication of the time you should be able to spend in the sun without burning. If you could normally be out in the sun for 20 minutes without redness, then an SPF 6 should theoretically allow 6 x 20 minutes, that is, up to two hours. This assumes that the sunscreen is reapplied after swimming and regularly in the heat about every couple of hours. An SPF of at least 15 is recommended initially.

More recently, an additional star rating of one to four has been provided on the packaging to show protection against UVA rays which cause ageing of the skin and sometimes an allergic, itchy rash.

Apply the sunscreen liberally remembering vulnerable areas such as the nose, shoulders, areas not often exposed to daylight and anywhere hair is thinning.

The Australian campaign slogan of Slip, Slap, Slop sums up the essentials:

SAFE SUN

SLIP on a shirt

SLAP on a hat

SLOP on some sunscreen

Getting sunburnt early on in the holiday can spoil your enjoyment for days after, so it is worth taking care to expose your skin gradually, especially areas that are usually covered up and only exposed when wearing a swimming costume (for more on this, see 'Common skin problems' on page 75).

HEAT

Overheating in hot climates can eventually cause sunstroke or heat stroke which could be fatal. It occurs when the body's cooling mechanisms cannot compete with overwhelming heat and consciousness is lost. It is important to prevent anyone from getting to that stage.

The body can adapt to hotter climates but it takes time and people vary in their speed of acclimatisation. For everyone, avoidance of heat stress is the key.

It is important to move slowly, staying out of direct sunlight where possible. In sunshine, ideally the head and back of the neck should be covered and loose cotton clothes worn. Lots of mainly non-alcoholic drinks should be drunk to compensate for the sweating taking place (alcohol, strong tea and coffee cause dehydration). More sweating increases the requirement for salt, but eating normally will usually provide adequate quantities and salt tablets are not recommended. Where exercising in the heat increases the salt requirement further, a little salt can be added to the food at the table, so long as adequate fluid is being taken to maintain pale urine. Dark urine is a sign of dehydration and the

best remedy is drinking as much oral rehydration mixture as you comfortably can (see page 88) or soft drinks.

Acclimatisation gradually conserves some salt by allowing less to be lost in sweat but fluid intake must still be maintained.

People who are suffering from heat stress may feel faint and sick with a headache and the skin may feel clammy. Later as the sweating mechanism fails, the skin may become hot and dry. Once someone feels ill from the heat, they should stay in the shade or preferably in air conditioning, and drink plenty of non-alcoholic drinks even if they don't feel thirsty. Oral rehydration solution is ideal (see page 88).

PRECAUTIONS IN HOT CLIMATES

- Stay out of direct sunlight wherever possible
- Wear loose cotton clothes and a hat to protect from sunlight
- Drink plenty of fluids (avoiding alcohol, strong tea and coffee as these cause dehydration)
- Do not take salt tablets. If required, small amounts of salt can be added to food, so long as you drink plenty
- Avoid vigorous exercise particularly in very hot and humid weather

Heat stroke

Heat stroke is a medical emergency. Immediate cooling and medical attention are essential.

HAZARDS OF TRAVEL IN COLD CONDITIONS

When planning trips to colder climates (including areas of high altitude and deserts at night) make sure that you go well prepared. Conservation of heat depends on good insulation and this is best achieved by adding layers of clothes which fit comfortably over each other. A good waterproof and windproof jacket is a valuable investment because heat loss occurs much more quickly if exposed to wind and rain. Remember to pack a warm scarf, hat, mittens and anti-glare glasses.

More serious trekkers may consider visiting a specialist outdoor clothing store where warm clothing can be purchased in lightweight materials.

It is generally well known that elderly people are more susceptible to hypothermia (a drop in body temperature which affects the body's ability to function normally), but certain illnesses may also predispose individuals to the condition. If in any doubt consult your doctor before travel.

Before setting out on long treks plan meticulously. Let a contact know where you are going, your route and when you plan to return. Check the weather conditions, access to emergency services, and plan for any other foreseeable dangers that will help to reduce risks.

Take sufficient clothes and equipment to cope should the weather change for the worst and wear well-fitting sturdy walking boots. Hot food and drink should be taken at regular intervals en route, and make sure that you take high-calorie emergency rations with you. Avoid alcohol because this enhances heat loss and increases the risks of accidents.

Fatigue and immobility also increase the risks of hypothermia, so recognise your limitations when planning excursions and try not to be too ambitious. Don't ignore in a fellow traveller signs of hypothermia which can range from complaints of tiredness, stumbling and slowed speech to uncharacteristic and sometimes aggressive behaviour.

Quick action to protect the person from further cold improves the chance of recovery. Wrap the casualty in dry clothes (making sure the head and face are protected), and move him or her to a sheltered area, getting immediate medical help if possible. If medical help is not available, getting a colleague to re-warm the hypothermic person through their own body heat (by removing all clothes and lying next to them in a sleeping bag) can be life saving. It is not sensible to take such action if this puts the other person's life at risk. Do not attempt to warm the casualty by placing too close to a fire. If the person's condition allows, encourage lukewarm (not hot) nourishment and drinks.

Frostnip and frostbite

Sometimes only the extremities (e.g. the hands, feet, nose and ears) are affected by below freezing temperatures, and this is known as frostnip or frostbite. Numbness and whitening of the skin are indicative of frostnip, and re-warming the affected areas by placing them in warmer areas of the body (e.g. putting the numb hand under the opposite armpit) is recommended. Avoid rubbing the affected area in an attempt to warm

it. To ignore these early warning signs is foolhardy.

Frostnip can progress to the much more serious condition, frostbite, with the real risk of loss of the affected part or threat to life. Immediate medical assistance must be sought to reduce the risk of gangrene and other complications.

FOOD AND WATER HYGIENE

Most of the agents which cause food poisoning from mild tummy upsets through hepatitis A to cholera and typhoid are transmitted in the same way. Somehow, bugs excreted (usually in the faeces) from one person are eaten by someone else. It follows that good personal and food hygiene will prevent a lot of infections.

The most important precaution is to wash your hands after using the lavatory and before handling food.

Food from street vendors and hotel buffets is generally best avoided as are certain species of tropical fish, because they can give rise to poisoning even when well cooked (e.g. ciguatera poisoning of barracuda and a wide range of tropical reef fish). Shellfish should be avoided unless cooked thoroughly.

Safe drinking water

Remember not to drink the tap water unless you are absolutely sure that it is safe. In areas where water may be contaminated you should also refuse ice in your drinks. Canned or bottled drinks sold under reputable brand names are available in most tourist locations. When buying bottled water, make sure the seal is intact because it is well known that some unscrupulous

vendors refill bottles with spurious water. In fact many bottles carry a notice to destroy them after use for this reason. Fizzy bottled water is less likely to have been refilled.

For those who are travelling in remote areas for prolonged periods, carrying bottled water is often not feasible. It is worth considering how you will purify water before you start your travels. There are a few options and some may be more practical than others.

Whichever method you choose it is essential to use the purest water supply that you can find.

If you are able to boil your water, this is the most effective way of sterilising it. There are many different opinions on how long water should be boiled for. Most references suggest between one and five minutes (even at high altitudes) to ensure sterile water. However, most experts believe that water which has just been brought to the boil is free from organisms that cause diarrhoea. For this reason tea and coffee are usually considered safe to drink.

If boiling is not practical, water can be treated with chemicals, such as iodine or chlorine. Commercial preparations such as tincture of iodine (2–2.5 per cent), iodine tablets or chlorine tablets can be purchased from travel clinics or pharmacies before you travel. Bacteria, the most common cause of travellers' diarrhoea, are very susceptible to treatment with chlorine and iodine. Other pathogens, for example, viruses or amoebic cysts, are not destroyed as easily, and treatment with iodine tends to be more reliable than chlorine for these.

Tap water can be treated at once, but water with solids (for example, river water with weed) must be filtered first to remove the debris.

There are of course a number of different water filters on the market. Some of these incorporate disinfection as well as filtration, making the process of water purification easier. Unfortunately, claims by some manufacturers have not been verified by independent bodies and it is worthwhile taking the time to investigate such claims thoroughly. Practical issues such as weight and size of the filter and maintenance should also be considered. Some filters are very expensive.

Correct storage of water is vital to prevent re-contamination. If water has been boiled, wherever possible allow it to cool in the vessel in which it was boiled. Make

FOOD AND WATER HYGIENE

Anywhere you suspect food hygiene standards are poor:

- Choose freshly cooked, piping hot food wherever possible and meat that is cooked through
- Avoid unpurified tap water and ice made with it
- Avoid salads
- Peel fruit
- Avoid shellfish unless thoroughly cooked
- Keep flies off food
- Avoid unpasteurised milk products
- Avoid ice cream unless from a reputable supplier

sure it is well covered and that the inside and rim of any bottles used are clean, allowing consumption directly from the bottle. Although it is worth trying to reduce the risks of food- and water-borne diseases, no precautions can completely guarantee protection from symptoms. It is sensible to know how to treat diarrhoea if it occurs (see page 88).

KEY POINTS

✓ Tummy bugs are the most common cause of ill-health on holidays; following simple advice can reduce the risks

✓ Know how to treat diarrhoea in case it occurs despite precautions

✓ Be aware of the dangers of excess sun exposure, especially in children

✓ Elderly people may be more susceptible to extremes of heat and cold

Accident prevention

ACCIDENTS

Accidents kill more travellers to developing countries than tropical diseases and are a major cause of health problems for holidaymakers wherever they go.

Obviously no one gets involved in an accident on purpose, but reckless or careless behaviour increases the risks. Conversely there are some precautions which can reduce danger to a certain extent.

- Do not drive when you're tired or after alcohol
- Do not drive or be driven on unlit roads at night in developing countries
- Check the condition of a hire car and the insurance agreement
- Use seat belts and put children in child restraints
- Hire a larger size of vehicle when possible
- Do not ride a moped, motorbike

- or even a cycle without a helmet
- Do not ride in the back of trucks or on the roof of trains
- As a pedestrian note from which direction the traffic comes
- Find safe places to cross the road
- Never leave children unattended near water
- Check the depth of water before diving in
- Check locally about sea currents or dangerous marine creatures
- Check the safety record of ferries and airlines if possible
- Piracy is a danger in some tropical sailing waters
- Remember that alcohol or drugs may affect your judgement.

There may be some potential hazards which you can't prevent completely, but at least if you're aware of them, you may be able to reduce the element of risk. Try to ascertain which areas of a town or country are safe to visit, but be prepared to hand over your valuables without a fight if attacked. Advice on political unrest/safety may be obtained from the Foreign and Commonwealth Office (FCO) before travel (see 'Useful information' on page 103); this includes updated advice on international terrorist threats and any areas that the FCO advises against visiting.

Hotels and self-catering accommodation may have unsafe balconies, lifts, electrical or gas appliances. Fire exits may be inadequately marked, so find out for yourself where they are and work out your route to them in advance. Camp sites may have poor security and be vulnerable to extremes of weather such as floods or sandstorms.

Sports risks may be increased by poorly maintained equipment – if in doubt, don't use them. It's probably best to steer clear of new and potentially dangerous sports unless you're sure that the instructors are properly trained and that there is adequate supervision and planning. Think about your own level of fitness too before undertaking anything strenuous or physically demanding.

IN SAFE WATERS?

Water sports are becoming increasingly popular, especially on the specialised activity holidays. As well as swimming, you can go water-skiing, canoeing, snorkelling, windsurfing, sailing and scuba diving. Sadly, this also means that more people are being affected by all kinds of water-borne infections, which can include tummy upsets, sore throats and skin, ear and eye infections. Occasionally hepatitis A (liver infection) or shigella dysentery can be transmitted in this way.

The rate of infection varies enormously but it can happen in all countries.

There has been much publicity about safe and unsafe beaches and whether bathing water is potentially hazardous to health. The number of British beaches passing cleanliness tests has almost doubled in three years; however, not all beaches comply, so ask if in doubt. You might also want to know whether there are any sewage outlets nearby. The local council environmental health department usually has this information. However, it must be understood that even at the best sites water quality fluctuates. A change in the current or weather can change a test result within hours so that natural organisms in the water or very occasionally diluted sewage from a distant coastal area can be found. Conversely, even where no faecal organisms have been detected, bathers may develop mild sore throats, ear infections and the like.

River water, swimming pools and whirlpool baths have all been implicated in causing infection at times. Very rarely a more serious infection such as meningitis may develop.

In a study of a gastroenteritis (tummy upset) outbreak associated with a busy swimming pool, it was shown that how long a person spent in the water and how much water they inadvertently swallowed were important risk factors.

A few organisms are resistant to chlorination although proper chlorination and filtration prevent most infections.

Whirlpool baths have been implicated in bacterial skin infections (an organism known as *Pseudomonas* species). River water in a

PREVENTING INFECTION

- Ask about the recent safety record of a beach (but remember testing may not have been carried out and, even if it has, it has limitations)
- Less crowded swimming facilities away from built-up areas and sewage outlets are likely to be cleaner
- Keep your head out of the water and avoid swallowing it if possible
- Try to teach children to do the same
- Don't let children swim or play in the water when they have tummy upsets and anyone with respiratory symptoms should avoid enclosed swimming pools. On hot days, especially when crowded, they can be the ideal environment for organisms to multiply
- Plastic shoes may reduce the incidence of plantar warts (verrucas) at swimming pools and infected cuts from outdoor swimming
- Avoid shallow natural pools with visible algae
- Whirlpools and swimming pools should be properly chlorinated
- Showering after swimming and drying thoroughly, including your ears and between your toes, reduces fungal and bacterial skin infections
- Ideally avoid immersion in fresh water near fields of cattle or where banks are inhabited by wild rodents, because of the risk of Weil's disease.

Although it's worth following these commonsense precautions, don't forget that the risk of infection must be kept in proportion; THE GREATEST RISK TO LIFE FROM WATER IS FROM DROWNING.

British rural setting may occasionally be dangerous as urine from animals (cattle or rats) can transmit a bacterium causing Weil's disease (lepto- spirosis). It enters the body through skin abrasions or nasal mucosa, and as it can be serious, it often causes concern to canoeists and windsurfers who have fallen into the water. Some people are more susceptible than others. Symptoms occur after about 10 days with a fever, chills, aching, vomiting and diarrhoea. It is usually treatable with antibiotics but there is a one per cent mortality rate. Approximately 50 cases a year are reported in England and Wales, but it must be said that only a relatively small proportion of victims can be shown to have been exposed to water beforehand. It is more common in most tropical areas, including the Caribbean and Hawaii, and is probably underdiagnosed in the USA.

> Teaching children (and adults) to swim and to respect the possible dangers of water sports must be the first priority.

Water-skiing boats should always have a lookout as well as a driver to watch that those in the water are not in danger from speeding propellers. Always wear a buoyancy aid for any water sport.

Windsurfers should also have warm suits (wet or dry) as learners can become exhausted if continually in and out of cold water. In the tropics, clothes to protect you from sunburn may be necessary. Beginners should not go windsurfing in an offshore wind unless a rescue boat is at hand as there is a risk of being blown out to sea.

Parasailing with a parachute behind a motor boat over tropical water looks spectacular, but it can be hazardous. Often the operators on the beach are disowned by the reputable hotels as they may have no insurance and accidents have sometimes occurred. Try to check on the level of care taken and

remember your travel insurance may not cover such activities.

Before you go scuba diving

Many people are tempted to learn scuba diving in resorts with crystal-clear turquoise water teeming with colourful and exotic fish. Increasing demand from travellers has put pressure on even small island resorts to offer this facility, but there may not be enough experienced teachers to meet this rapid increase in demand.

'Scuba' stands for **s**elf-**c**ontained **u**nderwater **b**reathing **a**pparatus. Less responsible hiring outlets will not check the ability of those wishing to hire and may offer only rudimentary tuition for novices. Don't dive unless you've had proper training (usually in a pool), the equipment is well-maintained and you know there are no medical reasons why you shouldn't. These may include chronic ear or sinus disease, asthma, bronchitis, heart disease, epilepsy and diabetes. In any case of doubt check with your doctor before you go.

Obtain local advice about any dangers from tropical fish, sea snakes or jellyfish.

Remember that snorkelling with a mask in clear water will often give you a wonderful view and, if used sensibly, will be much safer.

Fresh water hazards

In tropical areas do not wade or swim in freshwater lakes or slow-flowing rivers or drink water from them, however clean or clear they may look, because of the risk of infection with bilharzia (schisto-somiasis). Don't go windsurfing, water-skiing or canoeing on fresh water in an area where bilharzia is endemic unless you are certain that there is no risk. The infection is spread by the larvae of worms which burrow under your skin and can cause severe illness. Even if symptom free, you should get a blood test 10–12 weeks after a possible exposure to bilharzia-infected water because the disease is usually readily treatable.

It's a very good idea to avoid walking barefoot on tropical beaches, especially if they are fouled by dog faeces, and on damp earth in rural areas. You might otherwise risk infection with hookworm which can produce very unpleasant itchy rashes and sometimes more serious symptoms.

WINTER SPORTS

Unless you're already seriously fit, you can reduce the risk of accidents by getting some training in before you go. Exercises to strengthen rarely used leg muscles will be particularly beneficial. Invest in the proper clothes – you'll need a hat or helmet, mittens or gloves, warm socks and undergarments as well as the obvious ski suit. Good sunglasses, ideally with side protection, or goggles, will be necessary too. If you don't own ski boots, it is worth spending time on arrival to find comfortable ones that allow some toe movement. Adjustment of ski bindings must be done by an expert so as to protect against serious injury, and beginners will need advice on length of skis and poles.

You may feel you could do with some inner warmth, but remember that alcohol dilates the blood vessels of the skin so, while temporarily giving a warm feeling, it actually will cause cooling. And as with all sports, drinking alcohol increases the chance of accidents. Finally, before you are tempted to try your hand at tobogganing, you might like to know that it is responsible for even more injuries than skiing!

MOUNTAIN SICKNESS

There is less oxygen in the air at high altitudes. If you are suddenly moved from a low to a high altitude, you may feel unwell because less oxygen reaches your body's tissues every time you take a breath. These symptoms are called mountain sickness.

SYMPTOMS OF MOUNTAIN SICKNESS

- Headache
- Fatigue
- Shortness of breath
- Dizziness
- Nausea
- Loss of appetite

They can be prevented by going up slowly to allow the body to adapt to the lower oxygen pressure (by changes in respiration, fluid balance and the blood). So mountain sickness is basically caused by too rapid an ascent.

Mountain sickness can be unpredictable and can strike those who have not previously had problems at altitude. Fitness does

not guarantee protection and may even encourage a too rapid rate of ascent. However, some exercise and training before all active holidays is recommended for enjoyment and safety.

In the past when people had to climb up slowly there was more time for acclimatisation, but now holidays are offered with flights straight into airports at high altitude. For example, in South America, there are many organised trips which fly into La Paz at 3,577 metres (11,736 feet), Quito at 2,819 metres (9,249 feet) or into Lima at sea level but with rapid travel to Cuzco at 3,399 metres (11,152 feet).

Holidaymakers to East Africa may want to ascend Mount Kilimanjaro (5,895 metres, 19,340 feet) in only a few days. This summit is slightly higher than Everest Base Camp which is reached by serious trekkers but usually by more gradual means. Mountaineers obviously go higher, but such expeditions plan proper ascent rates.

The height at which symptoms begin varies from person to person.

ALTITUDE CHART

Area	Feet	Metres
Mt Kilimanjaro (Tanzania)	19,340	5,895
La Paz (Bolivia)	11,736	3,577
Cuzco (Peru)	11,152	3,399
Quito (Ecuador)	9,249	2,819
Mexico City (Mexico)	7,546	2,300

It is rare below 2,450 metres (8,000 feet) and most commonly occurs above 3,650 metres (12,000 feet). Trekkers, climbers and occasionally skiers can be affected.

Planning an itinerary with a slow ascent is recommended as it allows the body to acclimatise naturally and will avoid problems for many people.

Rest days should be built into high altitude treks, and the Himalayas Rescue Association in Kathmandu advises on safe schedules for Nepal.

When flying into any high altitude destination such as Mexico City (2,300 metres, 7,546 feet) or La Paz (3,577 metres, 11,736 feet) you should avoid physical exertion for the first day. Drink plenty of water or juice to maintain hydration (remember strong coffee and alcohol dehydrate), and don't smoke if at all possible.

Many people will feel a little light-headed or tired at first, but more severe symptoms can develop with headache, shortness of breath and/or nausea, and must be carefully observed. Mountain sickness can kill and it is vital that those in danger obtain a professional opinion or, if in doubt, descend to a lower altitude.

Some itineraries don't allow proper time for acclimatisation and the question arises of whether to use a medicine to help. Acetazolamide (Diamox) does help many people and your GP may agree to provide a private prescription (although the drug is not licensed for this purpose in the UK). It is important to understand that you can develop symptoms despite taking the tablets and, if so, you must still go down.

KEY POINTS

✓ Accidents kill more travellers than tropical diseases

✓ Holiday freedom and euphoria must be tempered by sensible precautions

✓ Alcohol has been implicated in a wide variety of holiday accidents

✓ Sports opportunities on holiday are increasing – avoid poorly maintained equipment and try to ensure expert tuition

Common health queries

Even though you may have thought carefully about the health aspects of your holiday and taken all the sensible precautions, it's impossible to reduce the risks to zero. Most people will have only minor problems or none at all, but if difficulties do arise, the important thing is to know what to do about them. If you are worried about any symptoms, however minor they seem, it's worth getting medical advice, just to be on the safe side.

COMMON SKIN PROBLEMS

With a little care and forethought, you should be able to avoid some of the skin troubles that are among the most common holiday health problems.

A priority must be to steer clear of sunburn, but sometimes the worst happens despite good intentions. Treatment is to stay out of the sun, preferably in cool air conditioning, and drink lots of non-alcoholic fluids. When only small areas of skin are affected, just those areas can be protected from the sun until they've healed. Calamine lotion is often soothing. Aspirin, for those who can take it, helps to relieve the pain and inflammation. Paracetamol in appropriate doses should be substituted for children under 12 and anyone else who can't take aspirin. When the sunburn is severe, you should seek medical help. Special blister dressings are now available.

When your feet are aching from sightseeing or have been rubbed by your shoes, try soaking them in warm, slightly salty water which is refreshing and may discourage infection of broken skin. On walking holidays much discomfort can be avoided by 'walking-in' hiking boots well beforehand and using seamless, moderately thick socks. If you develop blisters, stop wearing the footwear which caused them for a while if possible. Don't puncture a blister unless it is really necessary as the skin below will then be open to infection. If it has to be lanced in order to get your boot or shoe back on, at least temporarily, try to use a sterile needle, apply non-stinging antiseptic and a soft pad dressing.

In hot climates, and especially humid ones, minor abrasions and scratched insect bites can become infected much more quickly than at home. Antiseptic should be applied to all such minor wounds as a preventive measure. Any signs of infection which develop despite this should be seen by a doctor in case antibiotics are required. It's difficult not to scratch mosquito bites, but

this does encourage infection. Antihistamine tablets reduce the itching and swelling from bites but can make some people drowsy.

Another common itchy skin problem is prickly heat. It is caused by blocked sweat ducts and fine bumps can be felt on the surface of the skin in the affected areas. There is no real prevention or treatment apart from staying cool. Loose pure cotton clothes help, as does gentle washing in tepid water and patting dry without rubbing.

Sweating also aggravates fungal infections of the groin and athlete's foot. Again, loose cotton clothing will help as will open sandals. Keep the area clean and don't rub it hard. If you know you are prone to this particular problem, it's worth carrying some antifungal powder in your first aid kit.

Bright sunlight may cause a photosensitivity rash for holiday-makers on some medications. There is a wide range of drugs which can occasionally cause this problem and if you experience it, try to reduce your exposure to sunlight and seek help from a local doctor. Be sure you know the generic (proper) name and not just the trade name of any medication from home.

Most of the above skin problems are worse in hot climates, while chilblains and cold injury can be a problem for those on active holidays in cold climates. Wearing the right clothes and making careful plans in advance should reduce the risks.

LEGIONNAIRES' DISEASE

The Legionnaires involved have nothing to do with the French Foreign Legion. The disease is named after a group attending an American Legion Convention in Philadelphia in 1976 who developed a mystery respiratory illness. Despite the headlines of 'Killer virus' which usually follow such dramatic events, the cause was eventually identified as a newly recognised strain of bacteria now called *Legionella pneumophila*. It had not been identified before because it could not be cultured in the laboratory by the established methods. It is now known that it exists naturally in water and mud in lakes and rivers, and can grow in the water systems of buildings.

It has caused outbreaks after infecting the air conditioning and water systems of hospitals and office blocks in the UK and hotels in several western countries.

It can occur anywhere in the world.

Clusters of cases of pneumonia in returning travellers have been associated with hotels and apartment blocks in various areas surrounding the Mediterranean. The shower systems are usually implicated.

Continuous chlorination of the water and raising the temperature of all the circulating water to keep it hot usually controls the growth of bacteria. When this is done as a precaution, you need to be careful not to get scalded when using the hot water tap.

A person who has the disease, caused by inhalation of the organism, will have the symptoms of pneumonia with cough, shortness of breath, and often fever and chest pain.

Sometimes diarrhoea or vomiting occur early on. It is now treatable with antibiotics and so is usually only a serious danger to the infirm or those whose immune system is unable to function well. However, it is worth considering, or asking your doctor to consider it as a possible diagnosis, if you have symptoms of pneumonia after your holiday. See also SARS below.

SARS

Severe acute respiratory syndrome (SARS) was first recognised in March 2003. Cases arose in Guangdong Province in southern China and a doctor from the region travelled to Hong Kong and stayed on the ninth floor of a hotel there. At this point he was obviously acutely infectious and contacts from that floor of the hotel produced outbreaks, not only in Hong Kong but also in Toronto, Canada. Travellers from Hong Kong spread the infection to Beijing and it spread throughout many provinces of China. Cases were imported into other countries, including Taiwan and Vietnam. Recommendations to restrict travel (an extremely unusual step) to certain parts of China and other countries with evidence of spread were issued by the WHO, followed by the UK authorities.

Meanwhile only a handful of cases were imported into the UK with virtually no spread of disease from these cases. By 13 May there were 7,548 probable cases including 573 deaths from 29 countries. At the time of writing the outbreak appears to be slowing, but there is a potential for many countries to be affected and for there to be serious health and economic consequences. Health facilities, even in developed countries, can be severely stretched by the requirement for isolation and barrier nursing, so in developing countries there is even more potential for hospitals to be overwhelmed. Local quarantine measures are an important method of control and could potentially affect the freedom of movement of travellers.

The cause of SARS was unknown for some weeks. It is now thought to be a new variety of the normally mild coronavirus. The symptoms are high fever and a cough or difficulty breathing. Despite the highly contagious spread from just a few people who took the virus from country to country initially and the rapid spread to medical staff in hospitals and to other family members in the home setting, it appears much less contagious in most other situations, including casual contact in streets and airports. This is one of the many unknowns surrounding this newly diagnosed disease. However, one thing that is understood is that droplet spread is the primary route of transmission and therefore masks appear at least partially protective in the hospital and home setting. Although masks were recommended for a time in Hong Kong, WHO experts and the health authorities of other countries have not recommended masks on flights or in the streets.

Travellers are advised to be aware of the symptoms of SARS and those who develop them, especially if they are in or have returned from a SARS area, or believe they have been in contact with a potential SARS case, should seek urgent medical attention. More specific advice to travellers is difficult to formulate as a result of the evolving information about this emerging disease. To obtain current information on the outbreak and up-to-date travel advice refer to the WHO and the PHLS/HPA websites (see page 106). At this stage it cannot be predicted whether the disease will mainly be concentrated on China and gradually be controlled or whether it could reach epidemic proportions across the world. It is likely that precautions at international airports and around any local outbreaks will continue for a long time. WHO will continue to coordinate the work of international laboratories in the search for reliable diagnostic tests, specific treatment and, in time, a vaccine.

RABIES

It is a great advantage to live in a rabies-free island (but see page 81 about bats) and important to prevent the re-introduction of the disease to Britain. Many people feared that this might happen with the opening of the Channel tunnel, but the risk from France should not be over-dramatised.

In Europe, foxes are the main vector of rabies; however, distribution of vaccine on chicken bait dropped from helicopters in rural areas is helping to reduce the problem.

In general, dogs on the Continent are not rabid. Of course anyone bitten by a dog, cat or other animal in Europe must go for medical assessment and possibly rabies vaccine, because the domestic animal may have been in contact with a fox, but rabid animals are not common near to urban areas. Excellent treatment is usually available quickly (a major brand of rabies vaccine is French) and so human cases of rabies should be preventable – and although the course of vaccine is time-consuming and expensive, it is not unpleasant these days.

The real danger to travellers from rabies occurs in countries where the dog population may be infected and where treatment may be less than ideal. Many developing countries are included in this category. The Indian subcontinent and Thailand both have widespread dog rabies, and although dogs constitute the highest risk, any bite or scratch from a warm-blooded animal must be treated. An estimated 40,000 people die from rabies in India each year. This should not cause panic in visitors to that country, as treatment, including vaccine, given promptly after the bite should prevent development of the disease. However, treatment is easier and likely to work faster if you have been immunised in advance. Therefore if you are staying in a rabies country for some time or in a place where it would be difficult to get medical treatment, this option is worth considering.

It is worthwhile even though you will still need some 'treatment' vaccine (really it is prevention) after an exposure.

Many people still believe that rabies immunisation is painful and comprises many doses given into the stomach. In fact, the modern vaccine is virtually painless and is given into the arm. Most countries have an adequate version of the modern vaccine, even if not the very best one. A few rural areas in the African and American continents are still rumoured to have only the old-style vaccine.

There are still a few countries that do not harbour rabies in land animals (terrestrial) and these include Ireland, Australia, New Zealand, some Caribbean and Pacific islands, and some parts of Europe. However, any animal bite or scratch on holiday abroad should be properly cleaned and you should have a tetanus injection and antibiotics if appropriate, and seek medical advice as to whether rabies vaccine is necessary.

Recently, there have been isolated cases of bats carrying a rabies-like virus being found in Australia and a few in the UK. In 2002 a bat handler in Tayside, Scotland, was bitten by such a bat and tragically died from the disease. Rabies vaccine is considered likely to protect against this strain carried by bats and handling bats in the UK and all other countries should be avoided. Bat handlers should take precautions to avoid bites, should be immunised routinely and take further vaccine after a bite. Anyone who unavoidably has to touch a bat should wear gloves and seek medical advice if there is a chance that he or she has been bitten. Indeed, medical advice must be sought for bat bites in any country.

SEXUAL ENCOUNTERS

Many people see unexpected sexual encounters with people they meet while travelling as harmless fun and part of what makes holidays different from normal, everyday life at home. Their partners might be other holidaymakers or local people, but either way, it's important to bear in mind the potential health risks of sex with strangers. Remember that in some tropical regions, hepatitis B and HIV (AIDS) infections are particularly prevalent and are commonly transmitted during sex between men and women. In fact, it is thought that about three-quarters of HIV and AIDS infections in the UK acquired heterosexually can be attributed to sex with a partner abroad. Not all those affected were holidaymakers – some were people living overseas. However, the danger should be considered.

The risks of sex with prostitutes and drug addicts should already be well known. Despite this, sex tourism and sex on business trips flourish, particularly in parts of south-east Asia, and there have been tragic cases of HIV being passed from a husband who travelled to a wife who had never left home.

As well as HIV and hepatitis B, there are other, much more common, sexually transmitted diseases like gonorrhoea, herpes and chlamydia. The last has recently been implicated as a cause of infertility and highlights the possible long-term consequences of such an infection. Any open sores from sexually transmitted diseases increase the chance of HIV transmission.

Sexually transmitted diseases including AIDS are not confined to the tropics and there have been sad cases of infections caught during student trips around eastern Europe. In fact, no geographical area can be considered safe.

After a 'risky' encounter on holiday you can go for a confidential check at a clinic for

SAFER SEX

For those who don't choose the safest option of abstinence, the following guidelines should reduce their level of risk:

- Travel with your husband/wife/partner
- Try not to engage in casual sexual encounters
- More partners means more risk
- Prostitutes and injecting drug users are higher risk
- Using a condom reduces (but does not eliminate) the risk
- Carry condoms from the UK: they may not be easily available abroad, may be of poor quality, and in Asia may not be a suitable size for Westerners
- Safer sex means preventing semen, vaginal fluids or blood passing from one partner to the other
- Spermicidal creams used together with condoms may help to reduce viral infections, although over-frequent use can damage the skin
- Alcohol (and drugs) makes people more inclined to take risks without considering the possible consequences
- It's not always apparent from someone's personal appearance whether he or she is a 'safe' sexual partner

HOW TO ASK FOR CONDOMS ABROAD

Country	Proper name	Popular name
Spain	Preservativo	Gomma
Portugal	Preservativo	Camisa de Venus
France	Preservatif	Capote
Greece	Profylactico	Kapota
Germany	Kondome	Gummi
The Netherlands	Condoom	Gummi

sexually transmitted diseases and obtain treatment if required. Advice can be obtained from the National AIDS Helpline (see 'Useful information' on page 104).

ILLEGAL DRUGS

Any encounter with illegal drugs abroad may carry even greater risks – both legal and health-related – than it would at home.

The most obvious is that injecting carries a risk of hepatitis B and HIV, and taking recreational drugs may increase other risks by clouding judgement.

As recent media headlines have made clear, involvement in illegal drugs carries severe penalties, including death, in many countries. Some of those accused have pleaded that they did not know

drugs had been planted on them, so you need to be ultra-cautious.

- Avoid ANY involvement
- Do not take any luggage or packets through customs for others
- Do not leave your luggage unattended when items could be added without your knowledge.

DENTAL PROBLEMS

Reluctant as many people are to make a trip to the dentist, having to visit a dentist in underdeveloped areas overseas can be a much more frightening experience. Most worrying are the risks of infections, such as hepatitis B or HIV, from non-sterile instruments and needles, and poor hygiene procedures. But there can also be a risk of waterborne infections as a continuous water supply is necessary for dental procedures such as drilling.

Reduce the chances of having to visit a dentist abroad by having a thorough dental check-up before you leave. This may need to be arranged a few months in advance, depending on the treatment needed. For those going on prolonged trips, tell the dentist about your plans because it will be a good opportunity to identify any foreseeable problems.

If you have had a dental abscess in the past, it may be a sensible precaution to travel with a supply of antibiotics; discuss this with your own dentist or doctor before you go. Remember to take a supply of painkillers with you. Those who routinely take antibiotic cover for dental treatment may like to take a supply with them.

Dental emergencies

Warm saline mouthwashes may help to alleviate pain caused by infection, as may oil of cloves, until you can reach a suitable dentist. If you have a supply of antibiotics these can be taken as instructed by your dentist.

It is sometimes possible to repair chipped teeth, replace lost fillings or re-cement crowns and bridges temporarily by using materials that are available in dental repair kits (however, they can be tricky to use). These are available in travel clinics and some pharmacies. If you use one of these kits to re-cement a crown or bridge, make sure that the inside of the restoration is clean and try it to make sure it sits properly before mixing the cement. Make sure that the restoration is not loose once re-cemented, in case it is swallowed or inhaled.

If you are unfortunate enough to have a permanent front tooth knocked out, it may be possible to reimplant it if expert help is reached quickly. Clean it carefully by rinsing it in clean water. Make sure not to touch or brush the root.

Replace the tooth gently in its socket making sure it is the right way round and hold it in place until you reach a dentist. Immediate expert advice is essential because there is a very real risk of developing an infection, including tetanus, against which protection can be given.

If you are unable or unwilling to reimplant the tooth yourself, you should keep it moist by placing it in clean salty water or milk until you can get to help.

The sooner specialist help is reached, the better the chance of success, which decreases significantly if a delay of more than two hours occurs.

International hotels, embassies or consulates should be able to recommend a suitable dentist. Before undergoing treatment remember to tell the dentist about any medical problems that you may have as they will not be familiar with your medical history.

Where there are language problems it is usually possible to arrange a translation service through international hotels.

CUTS AND OPEN WOUNDS

Try to wash your hands before you deal with a wound. Even minor wounds such as scratched insect bites can go septic in tropical climates, so do your best not to scratch and apply some antiseptic to even quite minor abrasions.

Wounds should be washed in clean water, with a few drops of very dilute antiseptic liquid.

Any dirt left at the bottom of a wound, even a small puncture wound, can be a tetanus (or other infection) risk and medical help should be sought if you cannot clean it completely.

Cover the wound with a piece of

light gauze so that the air can get to it and hold the gauze in place with sticking plaster or a bandage. Keep dry as much as possible to help healing.

If the wound needs stitching together, get medical help which may also be necessary for wound cleaning, antibiotics and tetanus (or, in some countries, rabies protection if an animal was involved).

Coral cuts often become infected because of the tiny pieces of coral debris which cannot always be seen at once. The wound needs very thorough flushing with water at the time and antibiotics may be needed.

FEVER

A fever or a high temperature can be a sign of many diseases. Always check the temperature with a thermometer; normal is 37 degrees centigrade or 37°C (98 degrees Fahrenheit or 98°F).

Try to work out the cause of the fever, especially if it is above 38°C (101°F). Colds and flu are still the most common causes even when travelling. Sometimes bowel infections cause a temperature. Most of these will settle without danger in otherwise well adults, but any fever should be watched carefully and the patient should rest.

Emergencies to watch for are fever in someone who has been to, or is now in, a malarial area (not in the first week); it could be malaria even if there is diarrhoea. Neck stiffness and fever, usually with headache, could be signs of meningitis. Chest symptoms suddenly becoming worse could be pneumonia or SARS (see page 78). If any of these are suspected, medical help should be sought immediately.

Other reasons to see a doctor at once would be for any fever in children or elderly people, or in adults who have fever for 48 hours or who become confused, drowsy or seem 'ill', and any fever over 40°C (104°F).

While waiting to see the doctor, fever can often be reduced by tepid sponging of the skin, but don't let the patient get cold. Aspirin (for adults with no bleeding tendencies) or paracetamol for children helps to reduce a temperature. Drinking or sipping water is advised for conditions causing fever.

It may be helpful to have antibiotic treatment for those with a fever who are far from medical help so that self-medication can be used in an emergency until proper treatment is obtained. Some doctors are prepared to give a private prescription for this purpose. Others do not agree that 'blind' treatment is appropriate.

DIARRHOEA
Know how to treat travellers' diarrhoea

Most bouts of holiday diarrhoea are short term and inconvenient rather than serious. Replacing the fluid lost during diarrhoea or vomiting helps recovery.

Drinking lots of 'safe' water, juice or weak tea will help. Where these are not available, carbonated drinks from well-known manufacturers are usually canned or bottled in a hygienic manner, although in some situations they have more sugar than is ideal. For children and elderly people, it is even better to drink an oral rehydration solution which contains the right amount of salt and sugar to help to restore the balance. Commercial sachets are available at pharmacies. The mixture should never be reconstituted in a more concentrated form than instructed on the packet. The home-made mixture shown in the box below can be used where commercial preparations are not available.

Children become dehydrated quickly and medical help should always be sought early (see also 'Women and children only', page 36).

Fatty foods and alcohol should be avoided, but it is no longer considered necessary to stop eating. Moderate amounts of biscuits, bread and starchy foods usually shorten the illness.

'Stopper tablets' for diarrhoea will often help and allow the patient to feel better. They are given only to children under 12 on a doctor's prescription and are unlikely to be prescribed for very small children.

If the symptoms become severe with fever or blood in the faeces, or if the symptoms do not settle, then medical treatment should be sought. This is urgent if the patient becomes confused.

ORAL REHYDRATION SOLUTION

For adults this can be made as follows:

- One teaspoon of sugar and a pinch of salt in a glass or mug (approximately 250 millilitres) of safe water

- The drink should not be more salty than tears and can be flavoured with a little fruit juice

- Where vomiting is a problem, sipping the solution every five minutes may allow some to be absorbed

An antibiotic for self-treatment of travellers' diarrhoea or dysentery is sometimes requested before travel. In most cases, the infection will get better without it. However, if the correct tablet has been chosen it will shorten the illness, and so may be worthwhile for those needing to be well for an important event or performance or keen to avoid missing unnecessary days of their holiday. Although there is a small chance of side effects, these are unlikely with the short courses normally used.

BROKEN LIMB

Medical attention is required if you suspect a fracture. Meanwhile stop any bleeding by direct pressure with a cloth or shirt held firmly over it. Keep pressing until the bleeding stops. It may take 20 minutes or much longer.

Try not to move the injured part.

In an emergency, if the person has to be moved, keep the broken bone from moving by splinting it. Make a splint from the joint above the fracture to the joint below and pad it if possible. For a broken leg, it is easier to use the other leg as a splint, tied with bandages or shirts and padded between the legs with T-shirts.

GETTING ASSISTANCE

For any serious medical emergency contact your travel medical insurance assistance number. They will usually tell you who to contact locally. The insurance company may like to be contacted by telephone or fax before you run up any medical bills. If that is not possible obtain receipts from anyone you pay.

Other sources of assistance are hotel doctors; even if you are in an apartment, you usually know or can find out where there is an international hotel.

The British Embassy or High Commission may be able to advise about a local hospital or doctor, and offices of the major airlines and travel companies, and the local tourist office, may also know doctors who speak English. The telephone book may be useful to find the number of the main hospital, and it may mention a university or medical school affiliation which could mean that English is spoken. Outside main tourist areas, you may have to ask in the first police station you come to. Pre-planning before the event includes a phrase book to ask for a doctor in the local language.

There is an organisation, IAMAT (International Association for Medical Assistance to Travellers), which can provide a list of English-speaking doctors overseas who will see travellers for a fixed fee schedule. You can request the list on joining (no fee but donations encouraged) (see 'Useful information' on page 103).

For anyone travelling alone it could be worthwhile carrying a document on your person with your name, a home contact, your Embassy telephone number and your passport number, just in case you were found unconscious.

KEY POINTS

✓ Know how to treat travellers' diarrhoea in otherwise well adults; seek early medical attention for children, elderly people or those with a fever or blood in the stools

✓ In tropical climates, loose cotton clothing can help to prevent many common skin complaints

✓ Scratched insect bites and minor abrasions can become infected in hot humid climates; apply antiseptic to prevent infection and seek medical attention if it becomes necessary

✓ Any fever should be investigated promptly if the sufferer is in a malarial area or has returned from one (especially in the last three months, but even right up to a year later)

✓ Casual holiday sex could lead to serious infections including HIV and hepatitis B, or could result in infertility

Bites and stings

WOT-DA-YA MEAN...RUN FOR YOUR LIFE...

ANIMAL BITES

A bite or scratch from any warm-blooded animal (usually dog, cat, monkey or bat) in a country where rabies exists must be treated as a possible rabies risk (see 'Rabies', page 80). In the UK (or any other country), bat bites must be medically checked because of the death of a bat handler in Scotland in 2002 from a rabies-like virus.

Wash the wound thoroughly in soap and water, apply antiseptic and go immediately for preventive vaccine, and for prevention of tetanus and other infections.

If there is imminent danger of being bitten by a large carnivore such as a lion or tiger, rabies is unlikely to be uppermost in your mind. The advice, if about to be charged by a big cat – frighteningly difficult to follow – is not to turn and run, thus looking like prey, but to stand and face it, shouting and throwing stones in the hope of putting it off its stride.

It is far better to avoid any such dangerous situations; do not get out of the car to photograph a sleepy looking lion in Africa. It sounds incredible, but people have been taken in by their docile appearance. Similarly, big cats in UK safari parks or zoos are not partly tame even if they appear so. In recent years, keepers have been killed in British parks and zoos.

Perhaps surprisingly, buffaloes and hippos are more dangerous than lions, in that more people are attacked. Hippos are aggressive especially on land, if you are between them and the water. Despite their bulk, they can move terrifyingly fast. Buffaloes, especially lone animals surprised in the bush, are able to gore humans fatally and can also bite. Don't walk in the bush without a knowledgeable guide. If charged get behind or up a tree, if at all possible. Climbing trees is no escape from the grizzly bears of the American National Parks. Twelve people were killed in the 20 years to 1986 in the three major parks. Rangers will give visitors up-to-date safety advice, but it has been said that lying down pretending to be dead may be the best defence because bears prefer to kill their own food.

Chimpanzees and baboons can appear friendly and playful, and then deliver nasty bites. Obviously obtain medical help for such injuries.

INSECT BITES AND STINGS

A variety of diseases is transmitted by insect bites, and even when they are not dangerous they may be uncomfortable.

Some people have an allergic skin reaction to bites from mosquitoes, midges and horseflies even while on holiday in England and Scotland. The bite becomes itchy and the skin around it swells and becomes inflamed.

In acute cases infection spreads in red streaks up the arm or leg or even via the blood (septicaemia). Once this has happened antibiotics are required urgently, but it is better to reduce the itching earlier on and, therefore, the scratching and chance of infection. Individuals liable to 'swell up' with bites should reduce the tendency by taking antihistamine tablets. Antihistamine creams put on to bites work in the short term, but themselves may cause itchiness eventually. Calamine lotion is an alternative.

For older children and adults, preparations containing a little hydrocortisone will help to reduce the inflammation, and crotamiton to reduce the itchiness. Even better, reduce the quantity of bites by repelling the insects (see page 30) which can reduce the risk of disease carried by ticks, tsetse flies and sandflies, as well as mosquitoes.

Wasps and bees are not always deterred by insect repellent. Summer holiday picnics are a favourite time to be stung and their stings can of course be painful. If a bee sting is left behind, try to remove it by scraping it out carefully with a fingernail or knife (squeezing it with tweezers may release more venom). Holding ice over it reduces the pain, elevation of the part and/or antihistamine tablets reduce swelling. Painkiller tablets, e.g. paracetamol, may help. In a few people these stings can be fatal.

Sometimes these victims have had multiple stings, like bee-keepers, or receive multiple stings from a swarm. On very rare occasions, it can happen after a single sting because a serious allergy has developed which causes anaphylactic shock (collapse of the circulation and breathing difficulties); this can be fatal if not treated rapidly with adrenaline. Those who have had a warning reaction should carry a syringe with adrenaline (EpiPen) which can be injected in an emergency and enquire about medical desensitisation. Another way that a single sting can require emergency adrenaline and antihistamine is one at the back of the mouth which swells to obstruct breathing. It usually happens eating food or drinking outside and it is

essential to check each mouthful during al fresco holiday meals when wasps are around.

SNAKE BITES

Most people are terrified by the thought of a snake bite, believing that it could be rapidly fatal. Indeed there are estimated to be between 50,000 and 100,000 deaths a year across the tropics, mostly in agricultural workers. In the USA, with its rattlesnakes, there are about a dozen deaths a year and about half that number in Australia.

Despite the numbers in the tropics, few tourists are bitten and there are important points to remember for avoidance. Snakes do not attack humans unless cornered.

Not all snakes possess poisonous venom and, even when a venomous snake bites a human, very little may be injected. It is therefore important not to panic and rush about, which only speeds up the circulation of the poison. Venom usually takes hours, rather than minutes, to kill and so there should be time to get to help. Try to stay calm and reassure the victim.

Wipe the wound gently but do not suck or incise it. Try to immobilise the limb with a sling or splint, and transport the victim urgently to a medical centre (on a stretcher if possible). Tourniquets are more often dangerous than helpful. A description of the snake could be useful if anti-venoms are available. These should only be used by experienced people as they can cause serious allergic reactions.

Obviously prevention is paramount and snakes should never be touched even if they appear dead. Take care to avoid stepping on them, use a torch or stick to check the path is clear at night, wear shoes or boots in vegetation, and do not put your hand under any rocks, down holes or into dark corners in snake-infested areas.

Snakes do not only exist overseas; people do occasionally get bitten on holiday in the UK, although these bites should not be fatal. Prevention also follows the principle of not stepping on or cornering an adder or a grass snake. Go for medical treatment because infection, including tetanus, can be caused by either, and anti-venom may be advised for the poisonous adder bite.

SOME DANGEROUS SEA CREATURES

Although people fear land snakes, few have thought about sea snakes. They are mostly poisonous, brightly coloured and can be seen swimming in some tropical waters. Like their land cousins, they should be strictly avoided; they do not attack unless molested. The bite can be serious and rapid medical treatment is required. However, as with land snakes, remember that no venom may have been injected, although, as symptoms can take some hours to develop, the patient must be checked medically.

There are also venomous fish and jellyfish, mostly a problem in warmer waters, but among those which can be found around the British coast (e.g. Cornwall in summer) is the weaver fish. This produces a very painful sting when trodden on while paddling. There is a story that a trawlerman cut off his toes to get relief from the terrible pain.

In the tropics stonefish are among several species that are dangerous when stepped on. Some relief can be gained by long soaking of the foot in water as hot as can be tolerated, while waiting for medical attention.

Stingrays also lie in shallow waters and can inflict lacerations as well as release venom by flicking their long tails. Wearing shoes to paddle and swim reduces most of these dangers, although the stingrays can flick on to your legs, so walking cautiously is the only prevention.

Enquire locally about poisonous marine creatures, and what to look out for.

All wounds should be seen at a medical centre to remove any fish spines and to provide painkillers and any specific treatment that exists. Wounds are prone to infection if not cleaned professionally.

In tropical waters jellyfish can

kill by causing respiratory paralysis. One of the most dangerous is the box jellyfish. There have been at least 70 deaths a year in Australian waters. Mouth-to-mouth resuscitation may be necessary while the victim is got to medical help.

The tentacles must be removed without releasing more stinging capsules and vinegar splashed over the skin helps to inactivate them (box jelly fish only). There is specific anti-venom in Australia. Box jelly fish risk varies with the season and area around Australian and south-east Asian waters. Local advice must be obtained for each area for this and other poisonous jellyfish.

Portuguese man-o'-war jellyfish are also venomous, but less dangerous than the box species. It is sometimes found in British waters. Wetsuits and clothing when swimming reduce the risk of stings. First aid includes removing tentacles with tweezers, carefully without rubbing. An ice pack may reduce the pain before you get to a doctor for wound cleaning and possible local anaesthetic. Small children should always be medically checked.

Sea urchins, starfish and octopuses should also not be touched. Indeed local instruction on any dangers should be requested specifically if scuba diving or snorkelling.

Sharks are probably a more publicised danger in tropical waters, although deaths from shark attack each year are far fewer than the number of people who drown in UK waters.

It is not always known why a particular shark may attack a certain victim, but thrashing about or blood may attract them. Again, it is wise to heed any local advice.

Saltwater crocodiles are very dangerous, as are their freshwater relatives, and can grow to enormous sizes. They inhabit estuaries in south-east Asia, India, Sri Lanka and northern Australia. Do not swim in undeveloped areas unless you are sure it is safe.

SCORPIONS

Scorpion stings are far more common than snake bites. They are rarely fatal to adults, although southern India and Mexico are two of the areas where scorpion bites may be. Far more varieties are lethal to children and, in anyone, the sting can be excruciatingly painful. As with snakes, avoidance is the key. You should shake out shoes, avoid putting your hands under rocks, etc.

Once you are stung, very little helps the pain until you can get to a medical centre for an injection of local anaesthetic. There are anti-venoms for some of the poisonous varieties. Go for help even more urgently if a child is stung.

KEY POINTS

✓ Those who are allergic to bee or wasp stings should carry a prepared adrenaline injection (EpiPen)

✓ Avoidance is paramount in preventing snake bites, scorpion stings, sea snake and jellyfish stings

✓ Seek prompt medical attention for a bite or scratch from a warm-blooded animal in a country where rabies exists and bat bites in any country

✓ Bears, buffaloes, hippos and even lions may appear docile, when they can in fact move very quickly; heed all park warnings

When you get home...

- Continue any malaria tablets for four weeks (one week for Malarone)

- Tell your doctor you have returned from a malarial area if you become ill, especially in the first three months, but even up to a year or so after your return

- Mention that you've been on holiday and where (even if your doctor doesn't ask) if you see him or her about any unexplained symptoms

- Casual sex should be followed by a check at an STD clinic or by your GP

- Arrange to have a blood test, even if symptom free, after wading or swimming in African lakes or other schistosomiasis risk water.

AND THEN . . .

START PLANNING YOUR NEXT HOLIDAY!

Useful information

Age Concern Cymru

4th Floor
1 Cathedral Road
Cardiff CF11 9SD
Tel: 029 2052 1052
Fax: 029 2039 9562
Helpline: 0800 009966 (7am–7pm)
Email: enquiries@accymru.org.uk
Website: www.accymru.org.uk

Actively involved in policy-making and raising public awareness through research. Supports the development of local Welsh branches and refers to local groups. Provides general information on a wide range of issues including travel insurance.

Age Concern England

Astral House
1268 London Road
London SW16 4ER
Tel: 020 8765 7200
Fax: 020 8765 7211
Helpline: 0800 009966 (7am–7pm)
Email: ace@ace.org.uk
Website: www.ageconcern.org.uk
Travel insurance: 0845 601 2234

Researches into the needs of older people and is involved in policy-making. Publishes many books and useful fact sheets on a wide range of issues from benefits to care, and provides services via local branches.

Age Concern Northern Ireland

3 Lower Crescent
Belfast BT7 1NR
Tel: 028 9024 5729
Fax: 028 9023 5497
Helpline: 028 9032 5055
Email: info@ageconcernni.org
Website: www.ageconcernni.org
Travel insurance: 028 9023 3341

National headquarters in Northern Ireland offering information and advice on a wide range of subjects of interest to people aged 50 or over, including finding and paying for residential and nursing homes.

Age Concern Scotland

113 Rose Street
Edinburgh EH2 3DT
Tel: 0131 220 3345
Fax: 0131 220 2779
Helpline: 0800 009966 (7am–7pm)
Email: enquiries@acscot.org.uk
Website:
www.ageconcernscotland.org.uk

Offers information sheets on a range of subjects and a wide variety of services to elderly people through local support groups. Travel insurance: 0131 220 2778

Automobile Association

Fanum House
Basing View
Basingstoke
Hants. RG21 4EA
Tel: 0870 600 0371
Helpline: 0800 262 050
Website: www.theaa.com

Produces a publication *The Disabled Travellers Guide* via mail order. (Available free to AA members.)

British Red Cross Society

9 Grosvenor Crescent
London SW1X 7EJ
Tel: 020 7235 5454
Fax: 020 7245 6315
Email: information@redcross.org.uk
Website: www.redcross.org.uk

Gives skilled and impartial care to people in need and crisis in their own homes, the community, at home and abroad, in peace and in war. Refers to local branches who can provide equipment such as wheelchairs, commodes and bedpans on loan.

Department of Health (DoH)

PO Box 77
London SE1 6XH
Tel: 020 7210 4850
Fax: 01623 724 524
Helpline: 0800 555 777
Textphone: 020 7210 5025
Email: doh@prolog.uk.com
Website: www.doh.gov.uk/publications

Produces and distributes literature about general health matters including *Health Advice for Travellers*, also available on their website.

Diabetes UK

10 Parkway
London NW1 7AA
Tel: 020 7424 1000
Fax: 020 7424 1001
Helpline: 020 7424 1030
Textline 020 7424 1888.
Email: info@diabetes.org.uk
Website: www.diabetes.org.uk

Provides valuable advice and information for people with diabetes, whether or not members, and their families. Has local support groups. Members receive magazine *Balance*, free, six times a year.

Disabled Living Foundation

380–384 Harrow Road
London W9 2HU
Tel: 020 7289 6111
Fax: 020 7266 2922
Textphone 020 7432 8009
Helpline: 0845 130 9177
Website: www.dlf.org.uk

Provides information to disabled and elderly people on all kinds of equipment in order to promote their independence and quality of life.

Foreign and Commonwealth Office

Travel Advice Unit
Consular Division
Old Admiralty Building
London SW1A 2PA
Tel: 020 7008 1500
Fax: 020 7008 0155
Helpline: 0870 606 0290
Website: www.fco.gov.uk/travel
BBC Ceefax, page 470 onwards

Provides up-to-date, official, government travel advice.

Holiday Care

7th Floor
Sunley House
4 Bedford Park
Croydon CR0 2AP
Tel: 0845 124 9971
Fax: 0845 124 9972
Minicom: 0845 124 9976
Email: info@holidaycare.org
Website: www.holidaycare.org

Provides holiday advice on venues and tour operators for people with special needs in the UK and abroad. Publishes information sheets on overseas destinations. Offers professional consultancy service to the tourism industry. Minicom: 0845 124 9976

Hospital for Tropical Diseases

Mortimer Market
London WC1E 6AU
Tel: 020 7387 4411
Fax: 020 7383 4817
Helpline: 09061 337 733
Website: www.uclh.org/services/htd

Offers pre-travel advice, consultant-led clinics, post-tropical (travel) screening, a 24-hour travellers' healthline advisory service and fax-back information service, and specially selected travel products, that is, first-aid kits for backpackers.

International Association for Medical Assistance to Travellers

417 Center Street
Lewiston, New York
NY 14092
USA
Tel: 001 716 7544883
Website: www.iamat.org

Offers advice about health risks, geographical distribution of diseases and immunisation requirements for all countries. Maintains an international network of English-speaking physicians who can treat travellers in need of medical care.

John Grooms

50 Scrutton Street
London EC2A 4XQ
Tel: 08456 584478
Fax: 020 7542 2001
Email: charity@johngrooms.org.uk
Website: www.johngrooms.org.uk

Provides a range of residential care, housing, holidays and work across the UK for people with disabilities.

John Grooms Holidays

PO Box 36
Cowbridge, Vale of Glamorgan
CF71 7GB
Tel: 01446 771 311
Fax: 01446 775 060

Provides information on holidays in

the UK for people with disabilities and their carers.

Malaria Healthline
(London School of Hygiene and Tropical Medicine)
Helpline: 09065 508 908

Offers information about malaria. Calls charged at £1 per minute.

MASTA (Medical Advisory Service for Travellers Abroad)
Helpline: 09068 224 100

A 24-hour telephone helpline also providing written information. If travelling to more than one country please ring 01132 387578 and give the order in which you are visiting the different countries. Calls charged at 60p per minute.

MedicAlert Foundation
1 Bridge Wharf
156 Caledonian Road
London N1 9UU
Tel: 020 7833 3034
Fax: 020 7278 0647
Helpline: 0800 581 420
Email: membership@medicalert.org.uk
Website: www.medicalert.org.uk

A life-saving body-worn identification system for people with hidden medical conditions; 24-hour emergency telephone number to access members' medical information via reverse charge call. Offers selection of jewellery with internationally recognised medical symbol.

National Travel Health Network & Centre
Hospital for Tropical Diseases
Mortimer Market Centre
Capper Street
London WC1E 6AU
Tel: 020 7387 9300
Fax: 020 7383 4299
Helpline: 020 7380 9234
Email: nathnac@uclh.org
Website: www.nathnac.org

Newly established national helpline for doctors, nurses and pharmacists only, giving pre-travel information on vaccines; soon to be available on website.

RADAR (Royal Association for Disability and Rehabilitation)
12 City Forum
250 City Road
London EC1V 8AF
Tel: 020 7250 3222
Fax: 020 7250 0212
Minicom 020 7250 4119.
Website: www.radar.org.uk

Campaigns to improve the rights and care of disabled people. Offers advice on every aspect of living with a disability, including holiday planning and transport, and refers to other agencies for training and rehabilitation.

Sexual Health and National AIDS Helpline
Helpline: 0800 567 123
Website: www.playingsafely.co.uk

Free government helpline offering 24-hour confidential advice on HIV, AIDS and other sexually transmitted infections.

SOS Talisman

Talman Ltd
21 Grays Corner
Ley Street
Ilford, Essex IG2 7RQ
Tel: 020 8554 5579
Fax: 020 8554 1090
Email: sostalisman@btinternet.com

Produces a selection of identification jewellery available by mail order and through branches of Boots the Chemist. Medical details are supplied on folded pieces of paper, which are incorporated inside the various items of jewellery.

Tripscope

The Vassal Centre
Gill Avenue
Bristol BS16 2QQ
Tel: 08457 585641
Fax: 01179 397 736
Email: enquiries@tripscope.org.uk
Website: www.tripscope.org.uk

Provides comprehensive information for elderly and disabled people on all aspects of travelling within the UK and abroad.

Winged Fellowship Trust

Angel House
20–32 Pentonville Road
London N1 9XD
Tel: 020 7833 2594
Fax: 020 7278 0370
Email: admin@wft.org.uk
Website: www.wft.org.uk

Offers holidays at their own centres and overseas and respite care for people with severe disabilities by providing voluntary carers. Also arranges holidays for people with Alzheimer's disease/dementia and their own carers.

ORGANISATIONS COVERING INSURANCE AND TRAVEL ADVICE

Medicover

Tel: 0871 735366

Insurance company that will quote for travel insurance for pre-existing health conditions.

Folgate

Tel: 01202 668066

Insurance company that will quote for travel insurance for pre-existing health conditions.

Saga

Company specialising in travel for the over-50s, including travel insurance.

Trailfinders Travel Clinic

194 Kensington High Street
London W8 7RG
Tel: 020 7938 3999

Offers pre-travel advice with wide range of antimalarial drugs and immunisations. Doctor in the clinic daily Mon–Sat, no appointment necessary. Travel kits, nets and repellents available from the clinic and by mail order.

Useful websites

BBC Travel Health webpage
www.bbc.co.uk/health/travel

Information is also available on BBC2 Ceefax.

Health Promotion England
www.hpe.org.uk

Publishes fact sheets on immunisation and sexual health.

Health Protection Agency
www.hpa.org.uk

Incorporates the former Public Health Laboratory Service (PHLS); provides communicable disease information.

Scottish National Health Service
www.fitfortravel.scot.nhs.uk

Provides travel health information for people travelling abroad. Has current news, general advice for travellers and advice on malaria prevention.

Sun Know How
www.doh.gov.uk/sunsafe

The site provides a five-point Sun Safety Code and links to other related sites.

UK Online
www.ukonline.gov.uk

Government portal provides information on several 'life events', including travelling away from home. The 'Going Away' life episode offers links to advice on travel health and information on travelling with children and disabilities.

World Health Organization (WHO)
www.who.int/en/

Provides current outbreak and health information worldwide.

Worldwise Travel Information
www.brookes.ac.uk/worldwise

Provides country-by-country practical tips on health, safety, visa and currency requirements as well as information on local codes of dress and behaviour.

The internet as a source of further information

After reading this book, you may feel that you would like further information on the subject. One source is the internet and there are a great many websites with useful information about medical disorders, related charities and support groups. Some websites, however, have unhelpful and inaccurate information. Many are sponsored by commercial organisations or raise revenue by advertising, but nevertheless aim to provide impartial and trustworthy health information. Others may be reputable but you should be aware that they may be biased in their recommendations. Remember that treatment advertised on international websites may not be available in the UK.

Unless you know the address of the specific website that you want to visit (for example familydoctor.co.uk), you may find the following guidelines helpful when searching the internet.

There are several different sorts of websites that you can use to look for information, the main ones being search engines, directories and portals.

Search engines and directories

There are many search engines and directories that all use different algorithms (procedures for computation) to return different results when you do a search. Search engines use computer programs called spiders, which crawl the web on a daily basis to search individual pages within a site and then queue them ready for listing in their database.

Directories, however, consider a site as a whole and use the description and information that was provided with the site when it was submitted to the directory to decide whether a site matches the searcher's needs. For both there is little or no selection in terms of quality of information, although engines and directories do try to impose rules about decency and content. Popular search engines in

the UK include:

google.co.uk
aol.co.uk
msn.co.uk
lycos.co.uk
hotbot.co.uk
overture.com
ask.co.uk
espotting.com
looksmart.co.uk
alltheweb.com
uk.altavista.com

The two biggest directories are:

yahoo.com
dmoz.org

Portals

Portals are doorways to the internet that provide links to useful sites, news and other services, and may also provide search engine services (such as msn.co.uk). Many portals charge for putting their clients' sites high up in your list of search results. The quality of the websites listed depends on the selection criteria used in compiling the portal, although portals focused on a specific group, such as medical information portals, may have more rigorous inclusion criteria than other searchable websites. Examples of medical portals can be found at:

nhsdirect.nhs.uk
patient.co.uk

Links to many British medical charities will be found at the Association of Medical Research Charities (www.amrc.org.uk) and Charity Choice (www.charitychoice.co.uk).

Search phrases

Be specific when entering a search phrase. Searching for information on 'cancer' could give astrological information as well as medical: 'lung cancer' would be a better choice. Either use the engine's advanced search feature and ask for the exact phrase, or put the phrase in quotes – 'lung cancer' – as this will link the words. Adding 'uk' to your search phrase will bring up mainly British websites, so a good search would be 'lung cancer' uk (don't include uk within the quotes).

Always remember that the internet is international and unregulated. Although it holds a wealth of invaluable information, individual websites may be biased, out of date or just plain wrong. Family Doctor Publications accepts no responsibility for the content of links published in their series.

Index